Arizona: 100 Years, 100 Poems, 100 Poets
Published by Stuart Watkins
Edited by Hawkeye Watkins

Photo is of the entrance to the rodeo grounds at Sonoita, AZ.

© Copyright 2012 Stuart Watkins All Rights Reserved

Disclaimer:

Stuart wishes to acknowledge the creative effort of each poet. Some poems were modified to fit the format of the book. Many submissions contained intentional and/or unintentional misspellings, creative grammar, and other unconventional structure. A best effort basis was made on correct spelling, grammar, and structure while trying to remain true to the poet's intent. The views expressed may not be the view of Stuart, the editor, or the publisher.

The poems were intentionally ordered in a completely random method.

Photo submitted by Jay Dusard.
Bill, Skeeter, and Mack Hughes at the Diamond 2 Ranch, 1984.

Contents

Poems	9 - 231
Arizona Land, Ranch, and Farm Agents	232
Arizona Native American Tribes	233
Works Cited	234
Biographies	236

Author	Title	Page
Heather Ackerman	*Translucency*	157
Mark Adams	*Joy and Bliss*	196
Paula Ashley	*Van Gogh Paints the American Southwest*	92
Bob Atkinson	*Billy*	132
Mark Bahti	*There Was a Time When Poems Had Power*	146
Dick Bakken	*Going Into Moonlight*	43
Dick Bakken	*Javelinas at Sunset*	89
Sally Bates	*Say Cowboy To Me*	48
Jo Bates	*Sentinel*	97
Gerald Bigelow	*It No Longer Matters*	90
Gerald Bigelow	*Drifting*	96
Leonard Bischel	*Love*	12
Leonard Bischel	*The Elf*	95
Bonita Blankenship	*Yes, I've Seen a Javelina*	172
Philip Boatright	*Dusk*	88
Philip Boatright	*Sometimes Now*	88
Philip Boatright	*What Ken Bacher Saw From His Roof, Looking Down on the Mexican Bird of Paradise*	134
Gail Bornfield	*Desert Rain*	86
Harvey Bornfield	*For My Beautiful Wife Gail*	162
Christy Boughan	*Land That I Love*	51
Karen Bowden	*She*	85
Karen Bowden	*At Midnight With Eels*	102
Karen Bowden	*Apologia Poetica*	103
JoAnn Breul	*I Am Love*	138
Rhonda Brown	*Palo Verde*	84
Les Buffham	*The Belle of the Cowboy's Ball*	87
Les Buffham	*Arizona Wind*	99
Les Buffham	*One Footprint in the Sand*	100
Simmons Buntin	*Arc*	175

Author	Title	Page
Pat Bush	*These Hands*	56
Karen Call	*People Watching at Discount Tire*	82
Shawn Cameron	*The Echo of Jangling Spurs*	13
Betty Canavan	*The Holiday Horsemen*	223
Jefferson Carter	*A Centaur*	83
Lola Chiantaretto	*Come Wreck or High Water*	42
David Chorlton	*Night in the Wet Season*	16
David Chorlton	*Monsoon Days and Nights*	81
Charles Badger Clark	*Arizony's Probation*	33
Suzanne L. Cochran	*Rain*	141
Michael Cochran	*Again and Again*	164
Lisa M. Cole	*Wishbone Bush*	197
Matt Cometh	*Tom McConnell*	80
James E. Cox	*The Diet*	78
James E. Cox	*The Moth*	169
James E. Cox	*'Tis Time*	169
James E. Cox	*Hubris*	169
Mary S. Crume	*Caught in a Mirage*	137
Judith Curtis	*After the Monsoon*	79
Judith Curtis	*Time Travel*	94
Taba Dale	*Lone Flier*	165
Ingrid Dalton	*Arizona – Counties Without Boundaries*	76
Don Davison	*Lake Powell*	75
Don Davison	*A Mountain Man*	129
Don Davison	*Thunderhead*	158
Ron Dickson	*A Very Short Poem About the Day I Went into the Sugar Shanty Adult Novelty Shoppe to Buy an Inflatable Woman to Plaster Over for a Sculpture and Explained that I Needed a Model Without Hair Because Plaster of Paris Would Stick to Her Head*	71
Edward Dobson	*They Gathered Again*	221
Rod Drought	*Waiting For My Daughter At School*	70
Michael Dunn	*Wouldn't It Be Something*	73
Jay Dusard	*Spring, 1965*	74
Jay Dusard	*Southwestern Suite*	74
Jay Dusard	*Cactus, Sand, and Stone*	127
Richard Dyer	*The Coyote Song*	72
J. P. Ellsworth	*The Story of C. C. Hall*	176
Barbara Evans	*What Babies Need*	69
Jack Evans	*Room Eight and the Joshua Trees/The Graham Parsons Poem*	15
Erdeen Evertsen	*Friendship's Rose*	173

Author	Title	Page
Rolf Flake	*One More Rain*	66
Sandra Fortense	*A Gentle Breeze*	67
Ona Lesa Foster	*Phoenix in the Sky*	68
Ona Lesa Foster	*Haiku*	68
Ona Lesa Foster	*Ancient Dreams*	126
Robert A. Frost	*THE LAST GUNFIGHT*	193
Michael Gessner	*Washed Out*	208
Peggy Gigstad	*Speedway and Campbell*	65
Peggy Gigstad	*Monsoon Minute*	122
Dan Gilmore	*No Self*	64
Dan Gilmore	*First T.V.*	123
Michael Gregory	*Praxis*	62
Dean Guthery	*Arizona – You're the Best*	9
D. L. Guthery	*Arizona Castle of the Ages*	55
D. L. Guthery	*Arizona Stampede in the 40s*	98
D. L. Guthery	*The Cowboy Way*	104
Richard Hamilton	*Beloved Son and Brother*	61
Larry Harmer	*There's a Poem in There ... Somewhere*	60
Larry Harmer	*Mr. Grey's Cabin*	119
Joseph Harris	*Poems: What They Mean To Me*	188
Alana Helapitage	*Mother*	167
Archie Hoagland	*Farmer*	47
Archie Hoagland	*Desert Sunrise*	184
Carol Hogan	*Ocean*	227
Jim Hogan	*The Night New Orleans Drowned*	179
Jim Hogan	*Summertime in Tucson*	181
Richard Humphries	*To Some, A Life is Simply Being*	121
Richard Humphries	*Southwest Soliloquy by a Bard on the Border*	192
Kari Infantino	*Without You*	199
Felix Jaure	*Arizona*	59
Lisamarie Jelderks	*Mistletoe*	131
Lisamarie Jelderks	*Winter*	131
Earl Jenson	*Flight Poems*	52
Leila Joiner	*Leaving*	58
Leila Joiner	*Screwdriver*	117
Killian Kidrick	*To the Coyote, Wild and Free*	195
William Killian	*Exit 29*	39
William Killian	*Mothers Die at the Wrong Time*	115
William Killian	*There's Got to be a Better Place*	211
Ann Kuperberg	*Dear Wizard*	38
Ann Kuperberg	*Purple Passion*	226
Maggie Lawrence	*Early Morning*	37
M. C. Little	*DROUGHTS*	200
M. C. Little	*BOUGAINVILLEA*	201

Author	Title	Page
Aliya Ma Lynn	*The River Tidris, 1941*	116
Christina Martinez	*Out West*	107
Annie Maud	*The Dress*	202
Annie Maud	*The Box*	203
Charlotte Allgood McCoy	*Facing the Heat*	93
Melanie McCuin	*To the Novelist from Boston*	210
Kaitlin Meadows	*Five Hundred Years Ago*	35
Jonathan Messenger	*My Old Man*	17
Jonathan Messenger	*When the Purple Shadows Fall*	155
Debby Mitchell	*Curved*	32
Debby Mitchell	*Heat*	136
Bertha E. Monroe	*Way of the West*	30
Bertha E. Monroe	*Cowboy*	113
Sheila Murphy	*Toward a New Year*	130
Burgess Needle	*Tucson Night*	49
Burgess Needle	*Grandfather Antonio*	112
Regina Nelms	*Coyote Crucifix*	149
Shawnte Orion	*Vacancy*	29
Amy Ouzoonian	*On Letting Sleeping Dogs Lie*	205
Bonita Papenfuss	*This Season*	185
Holly Parsons	*Earth Speak*	10
Holly Parsons	*I Am Migration – Yo Soy Migrante*	111
Agnes Paulsen	*Time*	25
Agnes Paulsen	*Words*	110
Agnes Paulsen	*Immigrants*	159
Lyle Paulsen	*The Soft Fingers of Twilight*	161
Marge Pellegrino	*The Corner of Stewart and Lawrence*	142
James Robert Platt	*The Canyon*	28
James Robert Platt	*4 Corners*	108
Charles Portolano	*The Vastness of You*	124
Charles Portolano	*Coyote*	206
Charles Portolano	*Time in the Desert*	209
Hazel Ray	*Legacy*	144
Jen Reich	*Be*	150
Maria Rodriguez-Pope	*Today*	148
Cassius Sargent	*Dry Heat*	183
Larry E. Sarkis	*Generations in Arizona*	21
Larry E. Sarkis	*Arizona 100 Years Ago*	54
Barbara Scheidel	TIME TO REFLECT AND REDIRECT	186
PJ Scheidel	*The Man in the Door*	135
Helen Spencer Schlie	*The World Has Charms*	174
Marilou Schunter	*Mascara*	170
Elizabeth Doyle Solomon	*New Ears for Virginia*	187
Elaine Mickelson Stamm	*Weathering the Weather*	204
Mary Kay Stein	*Highway 101 North*	27

Author	Title	Page
Jim Tayburn	*A Heavenly Vision*	151
Fred K. Taylor	*Tohono Chul Girl*	53
Bob Temple	*Just Sittin'*	26
Bob Temple	*The Bronc Rider*	189
Jody J. Thompson	*A Quick One Near 4th Avenue*	140
Elizabeth H. Tilley	*The History Books*	222
Vanessa Vavrinec	*Insights of a Butterfly*	45
Marsha Ward	*Arizona Summer*	24
Hawkeye Watkins	*Coyote Whisper*	213
Hawkeye Watkins	*Have You Ever Heard the Sound of Nothing?*	216
Stuart Watkins	*A Tribute to Little Robe*	153
Stuart Watkins	*Time on Their Hands*	154
Stuart Watkins	*One God, One World, One People*	228
Stuart Watkins	*Two Birds in Cages*	252
mike. weisser	*Trickle (Rapidly)*	139
Carol Christy White	*Kokopelli Walking*	41
Jacqueline Williams	*Illusions of Farewell*	23
Jacqueline Williams	*My Fingertips Braille You to Me*	106
David Willing	*A Morning's Palette*	207
David Willing	*A Threaded Needle*	207
David Willing	*White, Weightless Light*	207
Marion Wilson	*Einstein's Girlfriends*	20
David and Judy Wood	*Lazy Lizard*	22
C. J. Wright	*The Surf*	143
Mark Young	*There Were Promises*	125
Luis Albert Yucupicio	*I Am*	191
Lisa Zaran	*Underneath*	11
Lisa Zaran	*Butterfly*	105

Dean Guthery

Arizona – You're the Best

I sure miss Old Arizona.
      Yeah, I miss it something fierce!
An' just to be back there again
      I'd give forty head of steers!
I miss the morning sunrise
      As it turns the sky to gold!
An' shows its earthly beauty
      As the cactus stands so bold!
I remember too the sunsets
      An' the stillness of the land!
As if the world of Nature
      Pauses for the view so grand!
I remember sippin' coffee
      As the sun sinks in the west!
An' I know that nights a'comin'
      So that most of us can rest.
But the wolves are howlin' lonely
      As they start their nightly quest!
An' the stars seem so much nearer
      Makes you feel like you're a guest
In this land of so much beauty.
      Arizona, you're the best!!

Holly Parsons

Earth Speak

Humanity – a word please
Self destruction on myriad levels
Necessitates intervention
Witness
Nature reorganizing
Every breath you take is and has always been
at our discretion
Every thought you think, every word you speak
appears within our collective mind
Devastated paradise
reflects your depth of thought and action
Iroquois wisdom sustains
Until evident
Cherish each privileged moment

Lisa Zaran

Underneath

All I wish
is to not be afraid.

What the rest of the world values
I find only a wrench
in my soul

and the quiet puzzle
of growing older
in my reflection.

Dr. Leonard Bischel

Love

I filled my heart with love one day,
And to all I met I gave it away.
Although I gave to all I met,
My heart is still the fullest yet.

Shawn Cameron

The Echo of Jangling Spurs

I sit in October's pre-dawn darkness
but much is missing.
There are no jangling spurs
nor booted heels across oak floors to tables set for ten.
There are no fragrant pots of coffee,
nor sputtering pans of meat...
Nor voices of men passing steaming platters that suffice 'till
darkness comes
and the ritual is repeated.

From my window I see no cold-backed horses silhouetted against
the barn light where chapped and booted men with heavy coats
flash fleeting outlines packing bridles, blankets, and saddles.
I see nothing... nothing but the twinkle of small lights that arc as
fallen stars on nearby hills.

I wait, but hear nothing familiar... no sound of horses' hooves echoing in crisp fall air carrying impatient, purposeful men bent on beating the sun to distant mesas.

No... only highways screeching with the sound of strangers speeding toward unknown destinations.

I find nothing of my world here, but, uncontrollably, it will find me. It will come to me when the first frost of fall glistens on October's golden grasses. I will look for men to come loping over the horizon... I will smell the coffee on the stove and I will listen... listen and wait for the echo of jangling spurs.

Jack Evans

Room Eight and the Joshua Trees/The Graham Parsons Poem

Back before the earth was dying,
back beyond the scent of reason
a voice was wandering
through the hard land
telling secrets to the rocks.
While hours dripped like falling weather
in this canyon of lost fears
I heard the vagrant sound of poison
lilting in the liquid sun.
As dreams deployed in shrouded deserts
and plowshares gathered at the gate
I listened past the sterile ticking,
watched the silence seek its level
where the cornered violence lisps in terror
where endless catches in the throat.
And now the voice transcends the tremor
to settle in the bones of stars.

David Chorlton

Night in the Wet Season

The roads leading into a storm
dip and wind
between a theatre of cloud and the grass
where sparrows wait for rain.
There's a brilliant light

in the sky
and a shadow moving in
as the mountains
rise to meet it. Heat has built all day

to the first lightning flash
that turns a deer's eye white
when she stops
to look back from her run
through the oak trees
whose leaves are silver

for a second. Rain gallops
uphill and down. Then the sun

returns as quickly
as it disappeared, and peak after peak
returns to its place
in time for the glow
that preceded the descent

into the time the owl
calls softly from its branch
and the Black Witch moth
arrives with a hiss

like a nail
driven through layers of dark.

Jonathan Messenger

My Old Man

Stand up straight, step out smartly, hold your head up...
    Always do the best job you can...
Eat your beans now and be grateful, do your duty...
    These are memories of my old man.

Born in Arkansas, his mother left him.
    His Missouri foster mother, she had to let him go...
Put him on a train in Lawrence, Kansas,
    Nine years old in 1924.

In Globe, he met his father for the first time...
    And began a life not meant for a child...
He stepped down off the train into a tragic story,
    In the wooly days back when the West was wild.

He and Grandpa walked from Douglas, Arizona,
    Five days on the old roads into Globe...
No food for those five days, and they grew weary...
    Depression days were tough old rows to hoe.

My grandpa broke his hands one night fightin' with a feller,
    Who tried to kill my dad at the hotel...
Then my dad went to work to earn the bacon,
    His childhood ended, near as I can tell.

He rode his bike for Western Union, from Douglas into Bisbee...
    Up that long old hill and back again...
He loaded trains, and trucks, and ran some moonshine...
    Dollars scarce as hen's teeth way back then.

In 1935 he joined the Army...
    Muleskinner, Ft. Bliss, Texas dust...
And he found the first great secret that he taught me,
    A man's a man who does the things he must.

My Old Man...
    He was my Old Man.

Pearl Harbor, Hickam Field, December Sunday morning...
    Sicily, Bastogne, and Buchenwald...
Sometimes, he would cry when he was drinkin'...
    Drownin' memories that boil and burn and scald.

Nineteen years she was and precious to his spirit...
    He was scarred beyond his years and far too wise...
She loved this man, my father, this wild and reckless angel...
    Whose halo was too dim to recognize.

Las Vegas, Nellis Air Base, a new baby...
    Trials and tribulations to transcend...
But through the years their love grew ever stronger...
    No trial of human life could cause its end.

Dry witted, some sarcastic, eyes a'twinklin'...
    Hazel in their mirth, and something more...
Searchin' for a rainbow in the desert of the spirit...
    An eagle lookin' for the room to soar.

A poet, and a prophet, and a pilgrim...
    With a restless heart that stood and built a home...
He tried so hard to tame that rolling stone that drew his spirit,
    Into that void of terror called *Alone*.

He laughed and cried and lived among us...
    And taught us by example – right and wong...
And my sister and I are blessed to have had him for our father...
    To raise us right he loved and labored long.

He asked me once how it could come in such a hurry...
    Seventeen to seventy-one in the twinklin' of the eye...
Five years more, my mama called one winter evenin'...
    He packed his spirit bag and said good-bye.

My Old Man...
        He was my Old Man.

Stand up straight, step out smartly, hold your head up...
        Always do the best job that you can...
Eat your beans now and be grateful, do your duty...
        These are memories of my old man.

As I recall his voice late in the evening,
        Tears of joy may tumble from my eyes...
And I hope that he can hear me – this man who was my Daddy...
        And I pray that if he can, he'll realize...

That I love him... and I miss him...
        This wild and reckless angel...
              Whose halo was too dim to recognize...

He was my Old Man.

Marion Wilson

Einstein's Girlfriends

It has recently been discovered
that the genius had a string
of girlfriends exploding
all around him.

Letters of long ago
tell of high voltage affairs
with a half dozen magnetic minxes.

These big bang babes
reached their boiling points
while gazing at the physicist's
electric hair.

They patiently listened
to his kinetic violin
with incandescent interest.

Vun of dem liked men
mit Cherman aggcents.

The force of these liaisons
caused the theory of relativity
to breach the black hole
of absolute zero.
It looks like E
wasn't so mc squared
after all.

Larry E. Sarkis

Generations in Arizona

How far back does my family tree go?
Let me think for a while then I'll let you know.
We've been around for a very long time.
The wide open spaces is for which we pine.
My family has always done good, we never cross the line.
We've watched Arizona grow and become a great state.
But, before that could happen, we had to clean up our plate.
My family was there during the Mexican War.
They watched the fighting and dying
and wished they could do more.
They helped in any way they could, do any odd chore.
Next came more white men with all that they had.
What they did to the Indians is terribly sad.
My family watched because there was nothing they could say.
The Indians were hunted and slaughtered in a way
That is still talked about today.
We watched as towns grew up all around us.
We saw as good guys cleaned up the towns of cruelty and lust.
My family always talks about the O.K. Corral.
What a fight.
It was hell during the day and hot at night.
Bad men got shot down, it was such a fright.
All we could do is stand tall, you see.
Because, at that time, my family was only three.
Next there were dams built to bring water to enrich the soil.
There copper mines discovered so men could earn money for their toil.
The cattle ranches, farms, and mines we watched come together like they were one big coil.
It was now 1912 and time for us to be a state.
I know you'd like to know my family name, which is still powerful to date.
We are none other than the great SAGUARO CACTUS of our state.

David and Judy Wood

Lazy Lizard

lizards dream lazy in dawn's ruddy glow
their eyelids flutter to challenge the sun
cactus wren heralds to creatures below
night's ebony ribbons coming undone

noon light blisters across sizzling sands
erasing spring's proof of promises made
last bits of shelter are stripped from the land
and bleached bones nestle in the scraps of shade

summer's heat swelter continues to rise
consuming all wishes for cooler days
the horizon holds only silver lies
and the twilight's reward of skies ablaze

always abounding life's victories won
like stories that pass from mother to son

Jacqueline Williams

Illusions of Farewell

She sought closure, healing,
an end to pain, final resolve,
but found a detour -
another isolated road.

Finally, her loss is buttoned up.
Why is she all exposed?
Now, it's sealed off,
yet something strange seeps out
staining her new disquise.

She has accepted it,
but find no surcease
from midnight thoughts.
Closure? Is there ever a resolve?
Or only new beginnings,
bravely planted
above the grave,
in open wounds,
nurtured well,
and fertilized
by love and tears.

Marsha Ward

Arizona Summer

Summer comes without gradual
Upward steps of heat.
It's here with sudden brassy sky
And lengthened day;
With sun-baked clay
Beneath bare feet;
With tan or reddened skin
Where falls Sol's ray.

Now men deny
Dame Nature's cooling way
And seek, with cream
Or roll, or spray
To keep sweat in.

Summer comes without gradual
Upward steps of heat.

Agnes Paulsen

Time

moments of now – moments in the past
    moments of the future
        all known as time
as soon as the present time passes
    it fades into the past
    no amount of money can retreive it
like words that escape from one's mouth
    once spoken can't be retracted
    acts done in haste can't be undone
today's moments vanish into tomorrow
    with an unrelenting speed
school bells ring – a vacation ends -
    a neighbor has a baby – a friend dies
all a kaleidoscope of life's journey.

The challenge

live each moment to the fullest
    life is a gift
be thankful for the smorgasbord offered
    friendships – opportunities – memories
        love yourself – reach out to others -
    settle for less than perfection.
time is priceless
    honor its value
    use it well.

Bob Temple

Just Sittin'

The sun's gone down, the day's ridin' done,
I've unsaddled, the bay's out to run.
The saddle's wiped down and it's hung up,
I'm just sittin' and pettin' the pup.

Collectin' my thoughts, it was a good day,
No problems, no losses, even found one stray.
Got the herd to better grass,
I'm just sittin', lettin' time pass.

If all goes good, herdin' ain't bad,
But then again, some bad days I've had.
An early wet storm can sure kill calves,
I'm just sittin', thankful fer all I have.

I've got three good horses, you bet,
A dern good saddle, a new felt hat.
Two pa'r of Levis, and Justins too,
I'm just sittin', havin' a chew.

Now I know that things can turn sour,
I could run out of beans, bacon and flour.
My horses could come up sick or lame,
I'm just sittin', watchin' the flame.

Too much thinkin' is hard on a man,
Better rest my mind all I can.
Tomorrow I'll need all that brain power,
Cause I won't be sittin' for 18 hours.

Mary Kay Stein

Highway 101 North

The eternal lure of California!
Sea glass, green grass, sand in a cuff
And sea kelp tumbled up in a rubbery vine.
Artichoke fields and a house made of crates
Goats and old boats
A pole corral
"We Buy Scrap Metal"
Pickers bent in half in green-gold fields
Cherry orchards
The Ford Store
Old barns and new cows
1970 Yellow Ford truck and its decades of dust
Cobwebs frame the mirrrors of days never seen again.
Pristine pines in a nursery
Natural old pines sway at the road
Daisies chin-high
And a field left alone so long
That a subdivision sprouted in it.
Land of sorrows
Land of Promise.
And always the Promise.

James Robert Platt

The Canyon

You are rock upon rock.
You are water out of stone.
      You are the dust of time.

You are the wind of thunder, the rain of the sun.
You are the aspen, the ponderosa, and the cottonwood.
      You are the condor embracing the rim.

You are the first step.
You are the last mile.
      You are grand.

Shawnte Orion

Vacancy

When you hit the pavement and bounced
from the sidewalk at Central Avenue
were you aware that your spirit still clung
to that seventh story ledge?
Where your whitened apparition
would haunt guests of those halls
into the next century.

Found making blood angels in the concrete.
No one could tell whether you were pushed
too far or if you were persuaded
to dive into eternity
by your own drowning heart.

A 22 year old actress from Los Angeles.
You likely checked in to the San Carlos

to ride that first Phoenix elevator
up to those first air-conditioned rooms.
Not because the water coursing through
this hotel's copper veins was being drawn
from a basement well directly over a sacred
Hohokam spring. Siphoning ancient water
from room to room. Energy flowing
between faucets and drains.

You likely checked in
to the Hotel San Carlos
in 1928, unaware
that even from the afterlife
you would be unable
to ever check out.

Bertha E. Monroe

Way of the West

You ask me why the love of the West
is so strong in this heart of mine?
When you can see it's passing fast
To make room for "progress" of mankind.

Have you seen God's plan unfold
in the blooming of each tiny flower?
They bloom, they wither, and they die
But the seed left holds great power.

God blessed mightily this West of ours
We call it the land of the free
And I'm blessed more than most others I know
As steward of land entrusted to me.

Have you ever ridden a rocky ridge
with wind and rain in your face?
Or come upon a tiny newborn calf
with his mother guarding their place?

Have you seen clouds all sizes and shapes
With linings of silver and gold?
Seen God's covenant in a beautiful rainbow
And heard plans from Him unfold?

On the back of a horse, life slows down
And peace envelops your soul
You rest for a while in God's precious arms
And His Spirit makes you whole.

Oh there's hard work in the way of the West
But lessons learned bless us all
Integrity, trust, and love for the land
Makes each of us ride tall.

Take your huge churches built by man
with doctrines to teach their way
Give me open spaces and the presence of God
And fellow believers beside me to pray.

I'm only a stranger in this earthly realm
My true dwelling is above the sky
But until the day Jesus calls me Home
Let the ways of the city pass me by.

Debby Mitchell

Curved

curved
this impatient throat curves like the bent road
cranes flying overhead never wavering
the lake echoing the blue veil of sky
your soft eyes surprised by the darkened burn
the hillside like overcooked toast, blackened
belief in the desert, ruined by this graying cloud

inhaling the recent fire, ash, all dank with burn
deep sips of smoke blurring the desperation
maybe the moon looks like this
flat, barren, scarred shrubs holding no green

inhospitable, vacant scrape of landscape
wildlife wide-eyed and gone
ingesting these fine particles of searing ash
fire suffocating slashes of scattered leaves
tumble with the breeze

a jackrabbit wildly, runs
down the road

on fire

Charles Badger Clark
Published in the Tombstone Prospector
Submitted and edited by Warren Miller

Arizony's Probation

Though the Utah man wears a dozen yokes,
    And Nevada stacks her chips;
They belong to the forty-six grown up folks
    And nobody minds their slips;
But young Arizony must do right
    And her people must be good,
So she'll walk in robes of shining white
    As she joins the sisterhood.
So it's long farewell to Old Nick's spell,
    To the guns and the doubled fist,
And the men can't score on the wheel no more,
    And the ladies can't play whist.
Quit your shooting craps – and you can't shoot craps -
    Nor indulge any reckless traits,
For a wisdom tooth ends our careless youth
    And we're going to join the States.

At the roundup camp when the stars peep out
    And the coyote tunes his harp;
You will find nice cowboys grouped about
    Playing marbles on a tarp.
And with lemonade their souls they steep
    Till the campfire light grows dim
While the cook reads "Pilgrim's Progress" deep
    And the range boss hums a hymn.

In the gloomy mines and the roaring mills
      Where the air was once so blue,
They have changed their ways and assumed the frills
      Of the W.C.T.U.
And the fireman sweats, but he plans to flee
      From the blistery fires to come,
And the miner just says, "Oh, dear me,"
      If the hard steel whacks his thumb.
Once Bill and Sam didn't give a damn
      But our wise men legislates
That we've got to be from our sins set free
      If we're going to join the States.

When our Arizony sashays forth,
      Dust white as her yucca bloom,
The fat old States to the east and the north
      Will remark, as they make her room,
"It is plain to see by your sweet face, dear,
      That you're strange to the ways of sin.
Plumb stainless is a rare thing here,
      And we need you bad. Come in."
So it's long farewell to merry hell,
      Blue smoke and the red, red paint,
And the first young lad hints we've been had
      Will be licked till he swears we ain't.
Now the water cart and an icy heart,
      For the Old Boys are tempting baits;
We'll be calm and cold and let on we're old -
      Now we're going to join the States!

Kaitlin Meadows

Five Hundred Years Ago

five hundred years ago,
did another woman look up
from this fragile land
and squint into
the layered glory
of a desert sunset
and say,
"this is mine,
> my little island of earth?"

did she call forth
the mother of water,
the father of fire,
to feed and comfort her children
and teach them the language
of her friends
> the deer, bear and coyote?

did she eat rain and drink moon light?
was her heart a divining tool,
like a pendulum swinging
from a silver cord?
did she place her sage bundles
wrapped in the webs of black widow spiders
as an offering
in the hollowed trunk
of a sycamore
> by the river of her dreams?

did she sleep on a thick pillow
of sweet moss
as the river's tide came throbbing
in and out,
pressing her face
into the furred side
of a bobcat
who purred
the same song
of the universe
that I am singing
to you
        now?

Maggie Lawrence

Early Morning

my house is haunted
I lie in bed and hear
my mother in the kitchen
making the breakfast coffee
she has been dead for 30 years

I've heard these noises
since my husband died last year
and abandoned me to
this empty house.
However, while I'm dreaming,
the house is populated
with my dear dead.

There's Lisa already
at her sewing machine
creating another whimsical dress.

Now I hear Bob hammering.
He has gone outside
to his workshop.
He must have waked up
with an inspiration, as Lisa did,
and is getting it started
while he waits for me.

I wish they would come
when I call them to breakfast.
My mother has vanished.
She didn't even make the coffee.

Ann Kuperberg

Dear Wizard

Can you make me forget
      planes crashing,
      people screaming,
      children crying?
Can you make loved ones return
      to share a bed,
      plan the future,
      hold us tight?
Can you make me safe
      from maniacs,
      harmful substance,
      intolerance?
Can you make the future
      bright with hope,
      filled with success,
      brimming with happiness?

Can you give me
      a brain that thinks of goodness,
      a heart that shows compassion,
      courage to forgive?
I yearn for the Yellow Brick Road
      to lead me home,
      where humans can live together in peace,
      accepting, understanding, respecting
      the differences that make us each special.

                Dorothy

William Killian

Exit 29

At Exit 29, I-19 crawls over
the romantic *Rock Corral Ranch*,
but when I visit there
I am in a quiet world all my own.

My visceral rhythms
unwind
as I remember
the history of this place.

I first entered
when the sweet matriarch
reigned with a smile
and proudly told her story.

I was summoned back
to marry off her daughter -
the daughter remained
and became the next sweet matriarch.

The *Ranch*
wrestles grief down to size,
lassos it by the neck,
tames it to heal the needy.

Then it tosses a party
into the garden
where the best of food and drink
blend a diverse people into one.

Music, laughter, and love,
children, *Pinata*, and memory
create a dance and celebration
that mix well with the dark.

The *Ranch Barbecue* scent -
aroma of beef, beans, and salsa
savored year after year -
is holiday, holy day for all guests.

As I walk toward the corral of cars,
drive past the bulky legs of I-19,
I cautiously make my way
to fragile places above, near Exit 29.

Carol Christy White

Kokopelli Walking

Kokopelli walks past the window
        dark as shades of shadow and dirt
He limps under a heavy pack
        puffs on a stolen cigarette butt

He smiles and nods at those who see
        the old god of this middle winter desert
Abandoned by his people a generation ago
        he wanders the city's dirty streets

looking for them in dark narrow alleys
        behind the trash at the liquor stores
up and down Indian School Road
        by the old sprawling VA hospital

During the day he sleeps in the park
        tucked under tall oleander hedges
no one sees him in the shadow and light
        with the prides of black and white cats

I doubt I'll see Kokopelli again
        not like that in his skin of dirt
hiding the gold of his lonely heart
        He's not looking for those who see him

Lola Chiantaretto

Come Wreck or High Water

Dismounting, they checked the proof
of what they had already known.
All that was left of the gelding
was hooves, hair and unbleached bone.
He'd been a good one, the red roan.

Just another casualty
of the harsh life in the Southwest.
Conditions could be less than prime
putting resolve to the test.
In spite of that, they had been blessed.

With predators everywhere
hazards of snakes and narrow trail.
Covered in rock, cactus and brush
only the hardy prevail.
Too rugged for those weak or frail.

The pair had spurred through the flood
having ridden the bronc named "Drought".
Facing their rival once again
they were set to stick it out.
If the cattle could just hold out.

Surveying land and cattle
concerned, he reached for his wife's hand.
With burdened heart and tear filled eyes
they prayed for all in the land.
Putting their future in God's hand.

So come wreck or high water
they had committed all their worth.
Facing the challenges each day
of hardship, surplus or death.
Hoping for rain to bring rebirth.

Dick Bakken

Going Into Moonlight

I didn't intend
to walk the old road

at midnight
but there I was, surprised

to see my faint shadow
on the dirt. I looked up to that

open moon coming down through
all the mist. A few more steps and there

lay my shadow across a jack rabbit
dead on the road.

I whispered
and reached and there waited

my shadow beneath
as I lifted from the earth the jack by those

silver ears. From beyond
the silhouetted hills, lightning

kept on washing up.
I love

that I couldn't
hear the night wings that passed before

my upturned throat. Only the muffled
roll of thunder far

from the other
side. I swung the jack

high away
into darkness while the next flashes

outlined us. And when I stepped forward, night
misting my face, the shadow

came with me.

Vanessa Vavrinec

Insights of a Butterfly

Hot, salty tears
running down my face;
My heart and minds'
uneven pace.

It's sadness and hope
and awkwardness alike;
This place between realities
unnerves my mind's eye.

It also numbs and calms,
though threatens to engulf -
As I teeter and totter
on its edges both:

One full of sorrow
One full of life;
One full of peace,
One full of strife.

Oh!
What to make of the clashing mind,
it with itself, again time after time.

A flourish, a fluster,
A float, and a boom.
One moment holds happiness,
The other impends doom.

But just because today,
Is not the same as the last,
And neither will tomorrow
Follow today's path –

It does not mean
That this makes the end…
It is simply another
Of life's many bends

Archie Hoagland
Published in The Collection

Farmer

Old blue shirt, buttoned to the neck,
rolled down sleeves, fastened at the cuff.
His strongest words were, "What the heck,"
bib overalls all frayed and rough.

Worn out shoes with a broken lace,
a pocket watch and old jack knife.
A farmer's tan on neck and face,
these things he carried all his life.

He only shaved but once a week,
he never had a lot to say.
If asked a question he would speak
and took a bath each Saturday.

Six days a week he rose at dawn,
in rain or sleet or sunny clime,
to work until light was gone,
when Mama called, "It's suppertime."

My daddy was a simple man.
My mama was a farmer's wife.
It was my daddy's only plan,
to be a farmer all his life.

Sally Bates

Say Cowboy To Me

If you say the word "cowboy" to me
It evokes a strong memory
Of men that I knew who were tried and true
And paid the cost to ride free

You can argue the word is a noun
An adjective, or a verb
What goes with the title is not just a word
It's a western degree that is earned

Like a PHD, BS or MD
There's a cost in dollars and years
And owning a ranch doesn't earn the degree
It comes with sweat, pain and tears

A degree that's earned the hard way
Through manure and dust every day
A true cowboy's heart is built, it's not bought
You can't pick one up that way

If you own a good rope and ride
And own forty acres of pride
That won't make a hand who rides for the brand
Whose face has the feel of rawhide

Don't say the word cowboy to me
Unless you know just what it means
A degree that was earned, a trade that was learned
On a diet of beef and beans

Burgess Needle
Published in Every Crow in the Blue Sky

Tucson Night

Bob's telescope evolved from
>plywood, discarded pipes
>and a hand-polished mirror.

Squatting, it was a
>benign, 3-legged spider,
>waiting in his back yard for my call.

Twilight on the road out of town found
>rows of hunter-citizens
>shotguns at the ready, staring
>skyward as we passed.

My rearview mirror showed the trajectory
>of wounded doves arcing gracelessly
>to greasewood and cholla.

Almost evening:
>near a thirty-foot saguaro,
>the tripod was set flat.

Past Horizon:
>final wink of rose is exchanged
>for dark particles that become night.

Present Music:
>pygmy owls hoot their requiem

Casually waving at constellations,
>Bob speaks the lines of a guide
>forecasting our extra-terrestrial tour.

A lunar reflection hurls
>Itself out through the eye-piece;
>nothing ghostly about it.

Craters like acne pit the moon's face.
The desert is still,
> perched mice pray the last pygmy owl will
> slip into extinction before dawn.

Bob aims first along Dubhe and Merak,
> Pointer Stars of the Big Dipper,
> until Polaris swims into view.

"Look!" he commands.
On a starry field I see a large, imperfect pearl.
Skidding across the pearl's surface
> a faint, gray dot inches along.

I step back as my brave wife bares her naked
> eye to untamed brilliance.

"Jupiter", Bob says, calmly. "The small spot
> is a moon's shadow."

My wife stares, silently, and I,
> aware suddenly of my isolation, wonder

"Am I truly part of this?
If I snap my fingers just so will that wave
> of sound nudge Jupiter?"

Behind us, a creosote bush shakes.
The death shriek of a mouse circles above.
Moths,
> in a delirium of light-madness,
> attack the brilliant pin pricks

of the night sky.

Christy Boughan

Land That I Love

The western sky blazes
With orange and pink.
I bid farewell to
The sun and I think,
There is nowhere else
On the whole of Earth
Where the sunsets are lovely
As the place of my birth.

Arizona has deserts,
Mountains, beaches, and snow.
Saguaro cacti choose
Only this place to grow.
There's more shoreline here
Than the California coast.
No wonder I love
Arizona the most!

Earl Jenson

Flight Poems

Poems are the ghostly
flutt'ring moths
whose desperate bumping
into porchlight
in this warming summer night
never ends.

Poets are the snatching
gulping birds
whose desperate feeding
in the scorched light -
in the swarming umber light -
never ends.

Reflex loathes to rhyme
or rhythm truth
when breathing in a bug,
swallowing a poem.

Fred K. Taylor

Tohono Chul Girl

Each day we were together
Me and my Tohono Chul girl
On the bus to school never
Did I dare sit next to you
Then off at the same stop
My eyes lowered, I had to watch my feet rise dust
As you went your way and I
Reluctantly went mine

I had the words all inside of me
If only I had the tongue to shape
The sounds
The mouth to give them voice
And the lips to speak to you
Thus it was those days of possibilities
Found me mute and unable
Social skills little or none
We only knew each other in my imagination
And now years later in this poem.

Larry E. Sarkis

Arizona 100 Years Ago

I think of a time when our state was free
Oh let me tell you what this means to me.
The water was free as it came down from the hills
The air was abundant with no toxins to be seen;
Yes the air and water were naturally clean.
The birds and the mammals were always around
Out on the prairies and mountains abound
Never to be seen in our small little towns.
When you went to a stream for supper to get,
You knew you'd get some, on that you could bet.
There are other things that we have for free
Let me add some more that belong to you and me.
There's a place in the north part of our state
I once called a hole in the ground, did I make a mistake.
If you wish to stand in awe for a day
Visit the Grand Canyon it will take your breath away.
Let's look at Sedona and what do we see?
The Red Rocks and mountains their beauty is free.
I think of Arizona 100 years ago with the mountains so high
And the valley so low.
The beauty of everything that is free
Is being destroyed by man because that is his creed.
I love our state and I wish to say
May you survive another 100 years; Happy Birthday!

D. L. Guthery

Arizona Castle of the Ages

Here's a Castle from the ages
    In a land nobody wants!
Where there once were many people
    Now there's only ghosts an' haunts!
Are there memories still floating
    In the ancient air around?
Of the natives who once lived here
    Where now there's not a sound!
The beauty of this ancient castle
    Bears upon my thoughts so strong
That I think I'd like to 'ave lived here
    Among these folks when they were young!!!

Pat Bush

These Hands

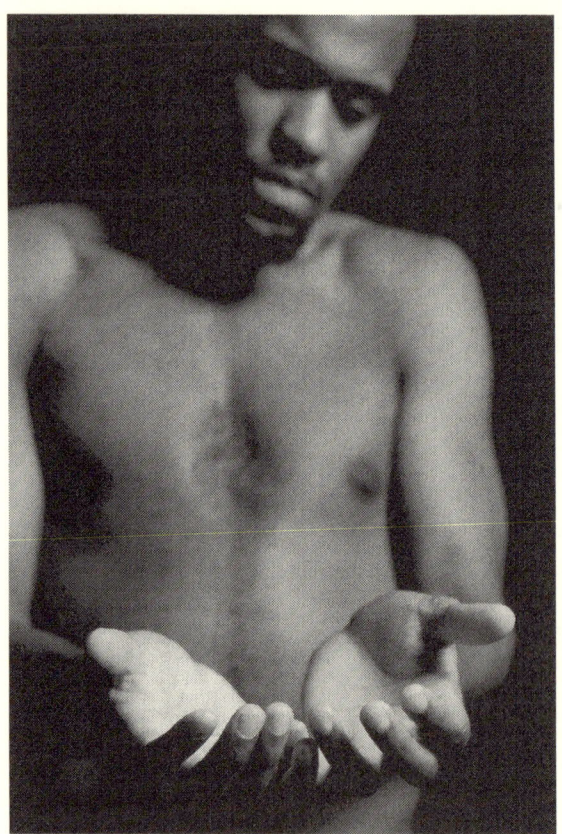

Photo submitted by Emily Hagopian

    These hands survived the hold
        of a slave ship.
    These hands became coarse and calloused
        in a cotton field.
    These hands held the baby taken from me
          when I was put on the auction block.

These hands covered my eyes at the site
    of a lynching tree.
These hands were cuffed and locked
    in a chain gang.
These hands bore the musket
    of a buffalo soldier.

These hands stifled my screams
    at an ethnic cleansing.
These hands carried the body
    of an AIDS mother.
These hands fed a starving child.

These hands hold the future.

Leila Joiner
Published in OASIS Journal

Leaving

I went to see you when you told me
you were leaving you met me at the door
my letters in your hand you stepped back
the room behind you empty of furniture
your belongings scattered in piles about the
perimeter I sat on the floor in the center
you prowled around me just out of reach
like an animal not quite trusting but fascinated
nonetheless drawn to the very thing you fear
we talked your circles drew nearer like
spirals nearer like a beast on a leash
winding itself around a tree I was the tree
you wound up next to me on the floor
on your back you let me touch you
I laid my head on your fuzzy chest
we were almost friends again

Felix Jaure

Arizona

In my south the days of winter are like those of spring,
and my nights clear as you've never seen.
My beauty will I share,
and the glory of God will be declared, as your eyes
become a witness to the vastness of my splendor.
For you shall see the magnificence of my deserts,
and all the life which they sustain.
My mountains shall you gaze upon, they ascend as a prayer come true
unto my skies so blue.
My beauty you will agree is as incense rising to the heavens,
and you will applaud my makers hand
as you behold the grandest of all canyons.
Glorious are my sunsets,
they are as the colors of the rainbow
far beyond the works of Rembrandt.
To my beauty there is no end,
I am Arizona, welcome to my land.

Larry Harmer

There's a Poem in There ... Somewhere

Standin' around at the Gathering,
      right after a session ends.
Just visiting and swappin' tales
      with a circle of old friends.

The stories all end the same,
      no matter who is there.
Someone pipe-up and says:
      "There's a poem in there ... somewhere."

"Ol' Slim was ridin' herd ...
      a rattler gave his horse a scare ...
Threw his hide up on a fence."
      There's a poem in there ... somewhere.

"Then there's the time when Shorty
      swallowed his mouthharp, square ...
After eatin' a plate of beans."
      There's a poem in there ... somewhere.

And the moonrise over the Superstitions
      that greets the night sky with flair.
The glow of the rocks in silhouette.
      There's a poem in there ... somewhere.

There's poetry deep in the rhymes
      of the stories that we tell.
There's poetry in the friendships
      that are forged here, as well.

We gather together to tell our tales
      and offer our feelings to share
And bask in a common bond ...
      There's a poem in there ... somewhere.

Richard Hamilton

Beloved Son and Brother

One day you came, born of love.
Sent to us by God above.
We shared your life, your joy and tears
for nearly 27 years.
From boy to man your dreams we shared
in joy and love, is all we cared.
Till that day your name did fall,
upon the roll that God did call.
Although your life, spared not this day,
your memory and spirit we daily pray.
Yes, your life from us, God has taken.
It was your trust in Him,
that you are not forsaken.
We feel your spirit in gentle breeze
through meadow, wild flowers and trees.
Your memory in our hearts doth dwell
for here we are for just a spell.
Our love in Christ relieves our pain
for soon together we will be again.
One day you came, born of love.
Sent to us by God above.

---

*In memory of
Thomas Robert Hamilton, STG2 USN
who died and went to be with his Lord
on September 2, 1991*

Michael Gregory
Published in Fiera Lingue

Praxis

Our dreams must be pragmatic – Aristotle

He had no badge except a gun
looking for the men and women
who stopped by my stand to ask for food
in a language I thought I understood.

They knew the Queen Anne's Lace, the spring
medicine plants, the evil-headed
creature curling out of the cabbage.
They walked among flowering herbs.

I gave them milk in cardboard bottles
(more than I knew I had left over
from feeding the cats) and some bread,
cheese and apples. A little girl

was with them, her eyes large and bright
with hunger, fear and unhappiness.
She said she didn't want to go on
like this, never knowing when

the man with the gun would reappear,
that all she wanted was to go home
where everything was as it was and would be.
She said that was what she wanted

no matter how often her parents explained
(and I, I admit, tried to help)
that place she thought she remembered was gone,
had never been, except in dreams,

for even there what wasn't known
was everything and everything
might change overnight as she knew
it had, you never know what might happen

which was why they had to keep going
now, to reach that dream place she
could come back to time after time
despite the change of everything.

Dan Gilmore

No Self

I've given up. The pilgrimage is over.
I've wasted too many years looking
for my one true Self. I've come to accept
that in the opera called my life there's
no top billing, only a cast of thousands,
all shameless amateurs bent on playing
me and scoffing at the idea of team play.

Some lie and cheat, some writhe in pain.
Some can't stop laughing. Some are men,
some women. Some would shoot their mother,
other would die to save her. Some hide
in terror. Others swagger like generals
inflated with grandiosity. Some are prophets,
some loose cannons. And I never know
who's going to show up next.

So, if you think of me, think of this gaggle
of bumbling actors who jostle and goose
their way forward to claim a moment
of your attention, a smile, a pat -
an undisciplined gathering with no scripts
and no plot, nothing except a puzzling
persistence seeking immortality
on the crumbling stage of imagination.

Peggy Gigstad
Published in Harmony Magazine

Speedway and Campbell

It is my lunch hour and my co-worker wants ice cream because it is Wednesday and she has decided that Wednesday is ice cream day. We walk across the parking lot in the chill wind when no one should be in the mood for ice cream. I would rather have hot chocolate or Starbucks but we maneuver through the six lanes of traffic, cross another parking lot, past the homeless guy's easy chair and the cart with his CDs, blankets, and a jug of milk. We finally see him on the steps leading to the dumpster and try not to wake him as we go by. He opens the slits of his eyes under his ski cap and gives us a peace sign. She gets her usual double chocolate chip cake batter and I try to think of a low-fat, non-chocolate, lent-appropriate choice which turns out to be better than I dared hope. It is a small miracle that sinless sorbet can be so good, like the taste of a second grade summer. We make our way back and I wonder if there are small miracles in the homeless man's life. Is it the music in his headset or some kind of liquor making the concrete steps a softer place to sleep? Is it feeling safe from the law, or his ex-wife or a distant war? Half of his favorite sandwich wrapped pristine in the garbage? Or maybe just knowing there is no one to tell him when it is time to sleep or wake or eat ice cream? His calves are tanned and dusty and the muscles are huge. I walk by him like a hardened New Yorker, like the Republican in my dad's DNA. If the loose bills in my purse were to find their way to be into his fingers, pastel petals of a gloved flower, would it be his miracle or mine?

Rolf Flake

One More Rain

All my life I've heard the refrain -
    "We'd sure be all right with just ONE MORE RAIN."
Most ol' cowmen have it tattooed on their brain -
    "Things 'd be rosy with just ONE MORE RAIN."
It's dry and dusty out here on the plain -
    It'd sure "green up" with just ONE MORE RAIN.
One thing there is that would sure ease the pain -
    I'm talkin' 'bout gettin' just ONE MORE RAIN.
I'm holdin' my breath watchin' the ol' weather vane -
    An hopin' and prayin' for just ONE MORE RAIN.
The cowman and cattle are sure under strain
    While they wait and watch for just ONE MORE RAIN.
We hope and pray that we don't wait in vain -
    We're dang sure needin' just ONE MORE RAIN.
Our cause for concern ain't hard to explain -
    Our livin' depends on that ONE MORE RAIN.
The cows'd give milk and the calves'd sure gain -
    If only we'd get just ONE MORE RAIN.
Of all our concerns, the one that's the main
    Is how we'd make it without ONE MORE RAIN.
As each dry day passes out here on the plain
    We're just one day closer to that ONE MORE RAIN.
All through the day our necks we crane -
    You guessed it – we're lookin' for ONE MORE RAIN.
We've had a fairly good year, and I shouldn't complain -
    But it'd sure be better with ONE MORE RAIN.
With this I'll quit 'fore you think I'm insane -
    'Cuz all I can think about is – ONE MORE RAIN.

Dedicated to Dan Jarvis, a fellow desert rancher. I don't know anyone who enjoys the poem more than he does.

Sandra Fortense

A Gentle Breeze

A gentle breeze blowing a fine mist
Through the cascading waterfall,
As the regal swan glides over the still waters
On the lake below.
A gentle breeze
Whispers through the tall stately pine trees of the forest,
And winds its way over and beside the desert cacti,
Gently tapping the flower petals
As they float down to earth.
A gentle breeze
Flows over the calm of the islands
Through the palms to the sandy beaches,
Slipping to the rippling ocean
As the sea gulls glide overhead.
A gentle breeze
Brings a new life,
A new day,
A new beginning.

Ona Lesa Foster

Phoenix in the Sky

(Metaphor for our Arizona sunsets)

The Sun is really the Phoenix bird, you know!

He rises every morning
from the violet and purple ashes of the East -
and flies majestically over the sky in splendor
each day to finally reach his fiery nest in the West.

Some evenings he settles down slowly into fire,
setting the sky alight with brilliant tones;

and sometimes falls like a stone
leaving Night to come on the stage hurriedly.

Ona Lesa Foster

Haiku

Splashing, dashing
down the mountain-side,
little, noisy brook.

Barbara Evans

What Babies Need

New babies need, well, everything!
But most of all a voice to sing
And read to them throughout the years -
Gentle sounds to caress their ears.

At first they hear a tender tone,
One that means, "With me, you're home",
But very soon it's so much more -
"You are the child that I adore!"

When sounds become the words they know,
Each new utterance helps them grow
And opens up the world that waits
Beyond your home and garden gates.

So sing and laugh and read and play,
Cuddle your little ones night and day;
Grace your babies with loving looks
And always surround them with lots of books!

Rod Drought

Waiting For My Daughter At School

Rare Arizona day.
The sky is an oil painting of
coarse strokes gray and black
dense with the promise of more.

Out my truck window
a damp, darkened tree with
a dozen puny grackles
scattered on bare branches.
Heads silently swivel
wondering what to do.

Only in Arizona can
a dimly lit day be this beautiful:
filtered light,
dulled color,
muffled weather – soaked sound.

Creosote permeates the air
and the waiting …
The grackles wait for the sun.

I wait for my daughter.

She climbs in my truck.
My double rainbow smiles.
She heard the weather report.
More rain will come tomorrow.

Ron Dickson

A Very Short Poem About the Day I Went into the Sugar Shanty Adult Novelty Shoppe to Buy an Inflatable Woman to Plaster Over for a Sculpture and Explained that I Needed a Model Without Hair Because Plaster of Paris Would Stick to Her Head

The clerk
was appalled.

Richard Dyer

The Coyote Song

The sun begins its slow descent,
        towards the desert floor.
The sky becomes a blaze of light,
        while brilliant colors soar.

Then shadows grow and cover all,
        the sunset fades away.
A multitude of stars appear,
        to end the fading day.

There comes a deep and eerie hush,
        as darkness settles down.
Then stealthy noises pierce the night,
        as creatures move around.

And then a lonesome wailing sound,
        disturbs the silent night.
A sound that stirs your primal fears,
        though nothing is in sight.

Then other voices join the wail,
        a chorus in full swing.
From barks to long and plaintive howls,
        a sad and mournful ring.

The coyotes howl is long and shrill,
        their voices fill the night.
And when the rising moon is full,
        they wail with all their might.

Their shrill crescendo fills the air,
        then fades into the night.
While distant packs take up the cry,
        beneath the moon so bright.

Michael Dunn

Wouldn't It Be Something

What if I could get away ...
    when the snow begins to fly?
The ranch won't be short handed ...
    I won't have to tell them why.
I'm wondering if I'd be welcome,
    if I could get away.
Wouldn't it be something,
    to get together for a day?

No one's getting married,
    no one passed away.
Just a thought we ought to visit,
    get together for a day.
We really don't need to,
    there's nothing we must say.
So wouldn't it be something,
    to get together for a day?

Do you ever stop to wonder
    why it is ... we are this way?
Memories have long since clouded,
    while time keeps slipping away.
Won't come if all's not right for you,
    I'll go me the other way.
But wouldn't it be something,
    to get together for a day?

The boss, he's a calling ...
    the sun is low in the sky.
I'll post this first chance I get,
    I gotta say goodbye.
Think about it, if you would,
    oh ... if there's any kind of way,
Wouldn't it be something,
    to get together for a day?

Jay Dusard

Spring, 1965

The tallow truck winch
draws my buckskin up the ramp.
I hate long goodbyes.

Jay Dusard

Southwestern Suite

Ice two inches thick
on the horse trough; brown colt bucks.
Great to be alive!

Blooming daffodils
ambushed by late April snow
better cowboy-up.

Cumulonimbus
shadows across dry ridges;
maybe it will rain.

Roundup circles sweep
golden country; weaned calves bawl
load 'em on the trucks.

Don Davison

Lake Powell

Cliff castles are rising,
cresting from the black-blue water
to the silver-blue sky.
What makes your heart stand in such stark relief?
Is it the memories of the ravens' shadows
cascading from cliff's edges,
or the salt cedar's graceful flickering
as they dance through days and nights?
What subtle undulations quake your feet
and force the calving of your children from your flanks?
They pile in small herds
then slide into the next sedimental shield
forming the new floor of the world.
There they remain,
waiting patiently to be sent skyward,
to stand again in stark relief against the desert sky.
And again I will ask,
what movement within the soul of the stone
still moves the mighty weight?
What gives us wonder from the deep?

Ingrid Dalton

Arizona – Counties Without Boundaries

Arizona's birthday's near:
One hundred years – oh hear, oh hear!

Fifteen counties you can count -
Most Native names and Indian ground.

APACHE County in Northeast -
Geronimo would have a feast!

NAVAJO with Hopis's catchy,
And there's more – like Fort Apache.

COCONINO's Grand Canyon land,
The Havasupai enjoyed their sand.

MOHAVE with three reservations
Has lots of land and preservations.

Nineteen-Eighty Three, LA PAZ
Was last county to get started fast.

YUMA is Quechan's land down South
Where Mexicans most likely browse.

"PIMA" expresses "River Men" -
No chance to see dry washes then!

SANTA CRUZ meets Mexico,
Still rivers there that really flow.

COCHISE, Apache Chief he was,
Great warrior for all kinds of cause'.

GREENLEE has large copper mines,
Combined with turquoise, all jewelry shines!

GRAHAM's known for flowing rivers,
Green countrysides it so delivers.

GILA has monsters that still roam!
Apache settlement's their home.

YAVAPAI's tribe – by all means,
Then growing maize, and squash, and beans.

MARICOPA's a busy area,
With Phoenix' daily traffic hysteria.

PINAL has mountains where they've met,
Apache Chiefs to Pow-Wow yet.

Lots of facts you could consider,
With history that lets you shiver!
Exciting things that happened here,
In cowboy land with farms and deer.

Land – just so beautiful and wide,
With sunshine, sometimes just too bright!
Saguaros and the Prickly Pear
Have everyone just glare and stare.

In fifteen counties without boundaries,
With nature so great, you've got to love these …
And people from all destinations,
AZ unites all of these nations!

James E. Cox

The Diet

I do not know why I said yes,
perhaps appease my wife.
And in my mind I hoped, I guess,
our world would have less strife.

She said, "We really have to try it.
It is the latest fad,
and if we both go on this diet
good health will soon be had."

Spare pounds had fused to flesh of late
and clothes no longer fit.
If eating less would shuck the weight,
why not ... try just a whit.

I did not know we'd eat just rice
morning, noon and night.
At least, you'd think she'd add some spice
and aid the taste a mite.

And all the foods I've grown to love
had now become taboo.
The t-bone steak from heaven above
had turned into rice gruel.

The precious drink, martini (dry),
I'd have as sun would set,
would be remembered with a sigh
(as close as I could get).

All alcohol ... a favored vice ...
could never pass a lip.
Warm sake (*which is made from rice*)
I could not even sip.

To meet her goal, I used my will,
and stuck to her strict plan.
But when she said, "Cocoa can kill,"
I grabbed a beer ... and ran.

Judith Curtis

After the Monsoon

It begins when a great wall of dust
sweeps in from the east
heralded by thunder drums
and jagged fireworks.
Then comes the roar of stampeding raindrops
that rage into unfettered torrents,
tumble over one another
into gaping, thirsty arroyos
that swallow the flood whole.

By morning the only signs of water
are damp shallow mud slides
smeared on slopes and pavement
mixed with gravel and debris;
and still humid air freshened
with pungent moist creosote.

On the hillsides saguaros
lift their arms in thanksgiving;
withered prickly pear swells fat
from last night's binge;
mesquites and palo verde are two shades brighter
Ocotillo bursts green; marigolds flash yellow;
lively lizards dart about
on cool rock surfaces
and skeletons of dead trees from last year's burn
resurrect themselves in nests of green Phoenician fire.

Matt Cometh

Tom McConnell

This grumpy old cuss had had his fair share of makin' dust
This Cowpuncher made of the west
His big hands are torn and battered
His face is a wrinkled map of time
His legs are bowed and his walk has slowed

Like the outfit trailer he is held together with screws and plates
Little oil here and there to keep him churnin' straight
This fearless eighty year old bronc stomper has savvy's all there
        is to know
Over years and through the tears he has earned an opinion on
        everything
This Cowpuncher that has lived like there is no tomorrow

Now has slowed but not come to a halt
He has taken up the craft of cowhand
His hands don't fit the strands that make the knot
As they work silent and swiftly on that tiny braid
Out comes a punchy little knot that tells the history
Of this Diamond in the rough.

David Chorlton

Monsoon Days and Nights

A storm across two countries
darkens the mesquite and ocotillo
but a blade of sunlight slashes through
the clouds into a valley
where green rain falls.
The mountains on the other side are lost
in thunder. Flags whip helplessly in the wind.
The border is a crooked line against the sky.
*

Beneath a flash flood of stars
a frog's voice sinks
into still water.
*

A crown of storms rests on the mountain ranges:
dark rain on the Huachucas,
gray light over the Mules,
and rumbling across Mexico's blue peaks
where a wet sky peels
away from the dry.
*

The San Pedro runs its muddy course
between tall cottonwoods.
A gray hawk's cry
moves across the silence like a nail.
*

An afternoon storm grips Miller Peak
at its tip, flashes a shower,
and flies away
with a wingspan as wide as two mountains.

Karen Call

People Watching at Discount Tire

It's Monday and I'm in a red-orange chair
by the window at Discount Tire
on Speedway Boulevard. It's time
to balance and rotate my car's tires.

I have a view of a dozen identical chairs,
a third are filled with men, the rest are empty.
I am the only woman here. The young man
on the end turns to look out the window and smiles.

I follow his gaze. A young female jogger
is bouncing down the sidewalk, pink bra
over band-aid black shorts, navel leading the way.
A three-foot tall dynamo is tearing up and down

the gray tile floor; no one but me cares.
Two men stand near the counter,
one reviews the Heat versus Lakers game
loud enough for non-sports enthusiasts to hear.

"Where wuz LeBron? Man didn't show UP!
Look'it Kobe, man, he wanted that win. Took it, too."
A man with a voice that bangs into the wall
stands at the counter. He wants to know

when his car will be ready. Two young men
in University of Arizona shorts saunter in,
leaves swirl around them. "Ma'am?" I hear.
People watching at Discount Tire is over.

Jefferson Carter

A Centaur

For laughs,
I imitate a horse,
lowering my bare shoulder
into the sand
of the arroyo, my wife
watching from above
& our son inside the blue backpack
watching while I roll, kicking
my hooves & neighing, husband
turned centaur, father
as some big animal.
The boy laughs
because his mother is laughing
& I lurch to my feet, shaking,
blowing through my nostrils,
feeling foolish,
but what's a family for?
Climbing back up,
I smell creosote & sage
& I understand the Greeks
who carried in their armor
a bag of spices
that smelled like home.

Rhonda Brown

Palo Verde

Evanescence tethered,
gossamer contained -
not given leave to soar,
it strains at root and soil.

And its gold sinks,
sheds its wealth of blossom
into yellow drift,
pooling and lapping
at the foot of the smooth green bark,

Earthbound ethereal
laying your carpet of bloom
on the desert floor
at my feet.

Karen Bowden

She

bares attractions like a circus barker.
Buy a ticket and she'll play the shell game
with her heart until she's certain nothing's
up your sleeve. Then you'll explore her Hall of
Mirrors. She'll closely watch your traces in
her twists. Are you strong? She might let you try
to ring the bell. Lift hammer high. But be
careful. If you're fooled by the surface flash
she half believes herself, if you really
thought to find heart in a shell, if you can't
deduce original from misshapen
twin, then you're bound to exit her fun house
down the bumpy black slide back into night
clutching a doll instead of a woman.

Gail Bornfield

Desert Rain

Clouds add a mystic beauty
Crested across mountain peaks
Folded into ridges and canyons
Resting, preparing for the pageantry

The darkened sky awakens
Bursting forth...
Clashing, crackling, banging
Lightning pounds the ground

Rain streams to the earth below
Water everywhere, running freely
Everything is washed anew
A freshness permeates the air

The scent of creosote
Signals renewal on the desert
Creatures spring to life
Scrambling with excited chatter

Bountiful branches sway
As plants display gratitude
In subtle shades of green
When it rains in the desert.

Les Buffham

The Belle of the Cowboy's Ball

Well, it was the Cowboy's Ball, the biggest, grandest one they'd had.
Looked forward to by each and all, 'specially the young, both lass and lad.
> The band was hot though the night was not, through the snow the folks had drove,
> And many would spend the night around that old pot bellied stove.

The hardwood floor was waxed and slicked to the benches 'long the wall,
And laughter filled the rafters of that country dancin' hall.
> There were punchers there and ladies fair from every ranch around.
> They'd come to dance and visit friends, some even came from town.

The lads were in their wildest rags and the ladies wore their best.
The talk would be for days to come how each and all were dressed.
> The fiddles sang and the guitars rang to the square dance caller's cry,
> And throughout it all, at the cowboy's ball, one young girl had my eye.

She was such a thing of beauty, possessed with style and grace,
As she whirled across the floor, a big smile on her face.
> She laughed and clapped and gave a bow at the end of every song,
> And when they played all the old favorites she would sing along.

With a smile wide as a river, she danced with every hand
That came for miles around across that snowbound land.
> When the ball was finally over, and they called out the last dance,
> I'd not had my turn with her and feared I'd lost my chance.

When she floated then into my arms, eyes shinin' like the mornin' dew,
And whispered then into my ear, "I'll dance this one with you."
> She looked across her shoulder then, at those faces long and sad,
> And said, "I'm sorry, guys, but I saved this one --- for Dad!"

Philip Boatright

Dusk

Will it rain or not
to clear our sight
strike the air clean
reassure with meaning
some brazen meaning
voices no matter what tongue
customs no matter how distant
until the found silence prevails
while we listen
listen

Philip Boatright

Sometimes Now

Sometimes now when I look out
there seems a flicker of movement
across the Yard
but no bird or lizard
shows itself
and then I see it is
the shifting of a leaf or branch
of a tree or bush
as it casts its own shadow
down upon the ground
nothing more
nothing less

Dick Bakken

Javelinas at Sunset

There's one

near that rock …
Yes see the rock

is another

stepping away -
Three. Four. Five.

All of us

still under stars
not yet visible.

Breathing

into this poem
that is gone.

Gerald Bigelow

It No Longer Matters

Your 1950s and my 1950s were not the same

You were buying spiffy new cars
Living in cookie cutter tract homes
Watching weekly episodes of Ozzie and Harriet

You were the new face of success

We were still the faces on boxes of pancake mix,
Cream-o-wheat, bags of rice and Abba-Zabbas

We ran on the railroad on the likes of the
Sunset Limited and the Super Chief
Changed your sheets in Pullman berths,
Serving your every need

You were free to move about the country

We continued to be terrified by public signs in
The South, saying, "If you can't read, run"

Experiences of my 1960s and yours were
Definitely not the same

You were asleep and
We were just waking up

The Brothers and Sisters that I knew in the 1960s
Were dedicated to getting respect

They were not running around with guns in their hands,
As many thought but with ideas in their heads

We lived in perilous times

Forcing us to shout in private places to be heard
And to whisper in public places not to be detected

Your life and mine were akin
To watching a double feature at a drive-in

Each screen showing a different movie

Ours in color
Yours in Black and White

It no longer matters!
It's the 21st century

Now here we are up the same creek
Neither of us having enough money to buy a paddle.

Paula Ashley

Van Gogh Paints the American Southwest

I steep green tea, sit at my table
listen to the haunting

native cedar flute and guitar
of Anthony Wakeman and Mr. Soon.

Yesterday we drove up the mountains
to Prescott above the heat in the valley

found the Courthouse Square covered
with tents and vendors selling crafts.

I wandered between booths admiring
beads and pottery and paintings of the desert

then gasped at flying tablecloths
hung from lines between trees -

tablecloths I had not seen since my stroll
on the shores of southern France.

I picked out a sunflower motif -
bright yellow and blue. Back at home

I went to the market for sunflowers
put them in a glass vase on a table

in front of the window where I sit
looking out on rosemary, bougainvillea

and a tall Spanish dagger.

Charlotte Allgood-McCoy

Facing the Heat

Well, PeeWee went a ropin'
Nearly every Sunday morn'
Come with us! His family cried.
Their pleas he did scorn.

He caught some corriente steers.
Roped them over and over again.
"I need the practice" He would say
While his kids were learnin' a hymn.

Well, PeeWee went a ropin'
Nearly every Sunday morn
He had to rope before the Heat
Dab a loop on an old steer's horn.

He became a top-notch roper,
But he never met the Lord.
He was big with his "drinkin' Buddies."
But with Jesus he never scored.

Well, PeeWee died a ropin'.
It was early on a Sunday morn'.
He tried to get into Heaven
But his pleas were met with scorn.

Your name is not in the tally book.
The Big Boss did repeat.
You spent Sunday mornings ropin'
Now you'll have to face the Heat!

Judith Curtis

Time Travel

The last of Orion fades into a gray dawn backdrop
for lance-stabbed agave skeletons, stark silhouettes
against the dim-lit sky.

Scrub trees and shrubs appear, anchored in schist
named after gods but far older than names.

Tangled flood trash caught in tossed saplings
is piled along the creek where it descends,
twenty thousand years a foot to the River.

Eye level from a sleeping bag, relentless ants,
a million years old, tunnel
downward with the gorge
doing detail work for wind and water.

Our stiff bodies stretch up to the day
through cool air with warm pockets warning
of heat to come with the sun
painting its way red down rock walls.

A jay, dusty blue, answers the clink of metal pans,
its caw magnified in the silence.
Wafting coffee draws squirrels rippling toward
a breakfast of jerky and dried fruit.

We contemplate how often this same water
has gushed down from the rim, cycled and returned;
who else has eaten here, carried full jars and dead wood
back to the terraced ruins on the hill.

We force sore feet back into boots;
stuff, heft and snap packs. Lizards erupt
out of fossilized mud where we tread,
hiking back up through time.

Leonard Bischel

The Elf

While strolling through the forest one day,
I chanced upon an elf at play.
He didn't notice my surprise
Or wondrous light in my eyes,
And quite ignored me, going about his play!

I quietly sat a distance away,
Hoping the elf wouldn't stray,
First he cut a small twig,
It really wasn't very big,
And with his knife began to whittle away.

It soon became apparent to me,
He was carving a flute, you see.
Soon those sweet elfin notes
Of singular beauty began to float
About the forest, coming from his tree!

The animals grieved breathily;
His story told of death, you see.
His pretty young elfin bride,
No longer there by his side,
Perished with the death of her tree!

I wept as I recalled that day,
When youngsters came just to play.
With an ax they found
Lying there on the ground,
Destroyed that tree and then went away!

All life is sacred, you know.
It starts small, and has to grow.
When you end its life,
Whether by hatchet or knife,
All life is dealt a terrible blow!

Gerald Bigelow

Drifting

When I see water,
a stream,
a river raging,
a silent brook,
a stormy sea,

I see the clarity of mind-flowing
unbridled,
unburdened,
unrestricted,

flowing like the sands of time through splayed fingers,

thoughts not constricted or firmly held in vessels of consciousness,

free flowing from place to place,
riding the waves of experience,

changing, ever changing,
with the rise and fall of aging tides,

drifting, ever drifting.

Jo Bates

Sentinel

The proud Ponderosa,
Stately skeleton sentinel,
Stands guarding comrades,
Fallen to the enemy – FIRE!

Passing time will see
New generations spring forth:
Juniper, sage, oak, fir, and pine.
Grass will cover the blackened soil;
Memorial garden for the fallen.
Victims of the enemy – Fire.

Still stands the sentinel,
Uniform stripped,
Lonely, proud, loyal;
Guardian of companions
Defeated by the enemy – FIRE.

D. L. Guthery

Arizona Stampede in the 40s

We were movin' some cattle – four cowboys an' I!!
      Down south of Phoenix – it was sure hot and dry!
Bud Baldwin, Don Whizinant, Bill Trabue and Joel Sublette
      On the bank of a big ditch – full of water? - you bet!
With a bobwire fence along the foot of the bank!
      We thought we had 'em but they were kinda rank!
Way off yonder we saw – a buzzin' here an' there!
      Like a bumblebee on steroids – a plane in the air!
Naw, he'll be no trouble – he's too far over yonder!
      But suddenly here he was – an' split our herd asunder!
With cows in the water – an' more thru the fence!
      A'hangin' that flyer – made a whole lot'a sense!
Had to rope fifty head – an' pull 'em out'a the ditch!
      We were callin' that flyer – what rhymes with rich!
With cows in the cactus an' down ever' road they could find!!
      We sure wanted to kick – that flyin' fella's behind!
Finally got 'em in the pasture where the boss wanted them!
      We're headin' back to the bunkhouse – feelin' kind'a grim!!
        As we moved silently along – headin' home at a lope!
One fella said, "I'd like to drag that flyin' fella on the end'a my rope!"
Another said, "I'd like to make 'im kiss a cow's behind!!
      An' that's what we all hoped!!!!

Les Buffham

Arizona Wind

Arizona wind, oh that Arizona wind
Keeper of her secrets, she comes and goes again
She pauses and she whispers of places she has been
The holder of dark mysteries, Arizona wind

If you're out on the desert where the tall saguaros grow
Pause there in your travels to hear the fair wind blow
She'll caress your sense, softly whisper in your ear
Secrets she's been keeping and now wants you to hear

Of the big mines down in Bisbee, the Copper Queen of fame
And one lost in the Mountains, Dutchman was its name
She speaks of the Anastasia and other men of old
Who vanished from the desert, their stories still untold

Of the pass they call Picacho (pee-katch-o) in eighteen sixty two
Three blue coats fell to a rebel yell 'fore the shootin' was all through
The trail of the Navajo and Canyon de Chelly (de Shay)
Tales of the Papago, that we still hear today

Of the purchase made by Gadsden for a new rail road ahead
Paid Mexico ten million, but the rails went north instead
Of the shootout in Tombstone where a few tough cowboys fell
And she knows what really happened at the OK corrall

Arizona wind, oh that Arizona wind
Keeper of her secrets, she comes and goes again
She pauses and she whispers of places she has been
The holder of dark mysteries, Arizona wind

Les Buffham

One Footprint in the Sand

Came the telegraph from Tucson
To say the Butterfield was late
There were passengers to board her
And should they have them wait?

The reply came from Dragoon Springs
That the stage had left on time
She should have been in Tucson
Without trouble on the line

Next day a search was mounted
From Tucson to the South
And the coach's tracks were spotted
Near the Jordan Canyon's mouth

They followed them back westward
Where they did then descend
To the bottom of San Pedro
Down by the river's bend

At the water's edge they lost them
And then the worst was feared
Tracks went into the shallow stream
And there they disappeared

Searchers rode the river bottom
'Til there was heard an echoed shout
They'd found a footprint going in
But there was not one that came out

The search went on for days and weeks
The army was called in
They rode out every Barranca
Where a stagecoach could have been

They never found another sign
'Til their quest did finally end
Was it revenge of the Apache?
As he moved about just like the wind?

Could it have been Mingus Colorados
Leader of a fierce Apache band?
They only found one moccasin print
There in the river sand

Karen Bowden

At Midnight With Eels

She watches as she turns
the man who watches her.
No trick to see

he imagines she
wants to dance, imagines
she wants to dance

naked, imagines her
in coral caves. She watches
as she turns the man

who watches her stretch
thin across a tight floor
toward what she hungers for –

sleep, her children
and a man whose desire
does not derive

from a woman who dances
with eels at midnight.

Karen Bowden

Apologia Poetica

I rarely know what is me
until I happen,
so I don't know what to hide

or what isn't me,
so I don't know where to hide.

I amuse myself by crossing
my arms over my chest
as if for protection,
but my heart is rarely there
where it's supposed to be,
sitting more often on my sleeve,
my shoulder, my right knee,
in the middle of my forehead.

I am surprised how genuine
what I am not can be
and how fatuous what I turn out
to be can seem.

D. L. Guthery

The Cowboy Way

The Cowboy way – at the end of day – as the evening shadows fall
Is to quietly rest – an' sometimes jest – with friends about it all
He talks with pride – of the horse he rides – of the work they've done that day
Of the Mossyhorn – that was surely born – to always slip away
He speaks of spurs – of colic cures – of saddles, ropes an' leather
Of floods an' drought – from nature's mouth – of wind an' sun an' weather
Of a buckin' horse – an' bulls of course – an' a cow pulled from a bog
Of roundup time – of a calf crop fine – an' a friend, his best cowdog
Of the Man upstairs – an' his earnest prayers – for strength to last the day
To give his best – to stand the test – for that's the Cowboy way

Lisa Zaran

Butterfly

The boy, by some miracle of deconstruction
has driven off again. She wishes he'd stay put.
She wishes he'd relieve her of the particulars.
She hates finding needles, tin foil burned black,
water balloons and the chronicle of clogged toilets.

At night her eyes close on a gondola of fright
and anxiety. She wishes she had a cigarette.
She wishes for the bygone days of long, summer
afternoons and mint ice cream, scent of chlorine
on his beautiful brown skin.

Strange how children demand so much of you.

And didn't he love her just the same? Without restriction.
Without constraint. And didn't he find her just
as beautiful as she found him? And wasn't the love
between them like the kiss of a rose to the edge of morning?

Mother and son.

Jacqueline Williams

My Fingertips Braille You to Me

My warm and sensing fingertips explore
dots 1, 3, 4, 5, 6, the "y" for you -
trace tenderness awaiting what's in store
when warm and sensing fingertips explore.
My fingertips urge you to want me more.
That lovers love with fingertips is true.
My warm and sensing fingertips explore
dots 1, 3, 4, 5, 6, the "y" for you.

Christina Martinez

Out West

Adventure you said
Straight flat road
Some thousand miles
Quiet heart, loud in my mind

A pile up of memories
In a too small wagon
Tiny eyes so weary
She turns her head to sleep

So familiar, the new faces I see
and somehow
so different from
all the places I know

James Robert Platt

4 Corners

"Just Gawd-awful nothingness
You don't think it's ever gonna end
Up road
Over hill
It's all the same
Monotony
Nothing
Seinfeld in real estate"
Crows the Phoenix, flapping aside its ashes

The Diné have a word (not topography, geography, nor geology)
If you aren't Navajo, it's unpronounceable
Oh, you may think you're saying it properly
But your inflection
Your interpretation
Will always be wrong
You don't possess the birthright
The history
The tongue
To say it
Let alone understand it
Its true meaning guarded by the People

A word to embrace the nothingness
Revere the vastness
Revel in its openness
Reveal true oneness
Acknowledge it is everything
A land painted and petrified
Arroyos and mountains
High desert and ancient dust
Wandering spirits and rocks
      Shiprock
      White Rock
      Standing Rock
           Window Rock
Unveiling

Canyons of depth and death
Filled to the rim by an arid tide of
Nothing
Everywhere
Embracing each and all

A land and a people's
Horizons defined by
Wind   thunder   horses and sheep

An emptiness that makes you
Appreciate what you have
        And envy what you cannot

Agnes Paulsen

Words

A single word or many words
> can alienate
> be harmful
> even tragic

Put down words
> pierce the self image like a sharp needle
> puncture the core of the inner self
> painfully stab one's inmost being

Reprimanding words
> crush self worth
> invite hatred and anger
> create antagonism

A single word or many words
> can support
> invite friendship
> spread joy like magic

Benevolent words
> bridge differences
> trigger positive responses
> serve as a vehicle of love

A single word or many words
> can be like untended ugly weeds along a roadside
> or a nurtured garden of beautiful blooming flowers.

Holly A. Parsons

I Am Migration – Yo Soy Migrante

Life
Vida
Travel as water
Viajando como el agua
Alive when flowing
Viva cuando fluye
Rancid if stagnant
Rancio si se estanca
Indigenous birthright
Indigena de Nacimiento
Enchanted Earth
Tierra encantada
Reflect our dream
Refleja nuestros sueños
Open borders
Fronteras abiertas
Steward everything
Cuidador de todo
Protect life
Protejo la vida
Treasure children
Valora los niños
Grateful for each breath we borrow
Agradecidos por cada respiro que tomamos prestado

Burgess Needle

Grandfather Antonio

Alfredo said, "Let me tell you
my grandfather, Antonio, is one weird dude."
Twisting and turning the tale came out
      how the old man and his friends
      never forgot their birth city, Hermosillo.
Truth is, he got to where he is by walking.
Man, he covered it all.
Right through Sonora,
      trailing funerals!
Menudo! Free booze!
He'd hit a town, find out
      if anyone'd died, and go over
      for the wake. All the women
      in *luto* outside while the men passed
      mescal and watched a fire;
Then, back inside to sit and drink some more.
Alfredo's mother said, "Tata didn't walk here,
      he waked here!"
That's when Antonio himself limped into the room.
When I asked him about that, he told me
      of a wake in Bahia Kino
      when the new corpse twitched
      and stared, he thought, at him
Making him drop his glass and leap
      out a window   badly.
"My leg never healed," he grimaced,
      "so I still limp to this day,
      hardly ever drink Mescal and
I never, ever, go to wakes."

Bertha E. Monroe

"Cowboy"

I was introduced to a young man one day
      "He's a cowboy" is what was said
He shook my hand and asked, "How ya doin'?"
      Then I stood back and scratched my head

I've been around quite a number of years
      This face can attest to that fact
And if this is a <u>cowboy</u>, as I knew them
      Then my hide to the wall be tacked!

For one thing, he's way short on manners
      Seemed 'twas a favor to just shake his hand
A <u>cowboy</u> would sure have tipped his hat
      To my age, and that I wore the female brand.

And then he starts talkin' about Jesus
      With no reverence for the Father's Son
This kid kept taking the Lord's name in vain
      And his mouth just continued to run.

I could feel my neck getting' kinda hot
      'Cause it was my Lord he spoke about
Was telling myself "rebuke gently with love"
      But really wanted to give him a clout!

Then up stepped a man of quiet demeanor
      And said, "Son, you just stepped over the line
For you're in the presence of women folk
      And you're profaning the Savior of mine!

Well, that young man was some deflated
      But he knew it must be set right
And I saw then that somewhere, someone
      Had done a lot of praying at night.

For this young Cowboy held his hat to his heart
        Bowed slightly and said, Excuse me please
For I was raised better than what I just showed
        And will spend some time on my knees!"

I thank God for folks who keep praying
        And for those who take a quiet stand
And by their example lead the young ones
        In the way and means of becoming a man.

William Killian
Published in All the Faces I Have Been

Mothers Die at the Wrong Time

He said I went to my mother's funeral in chains
at one of those meetings
where healing happens through talk.

We knew enough to know his grief,
how much he loved his mother,
but he talked on and on,
moving from honest poetry to sermons
which is where you always end up
if you talk too much and wear chains
to your mother's funeral.

Aliya Ma Lynn

The River Tidris, 1941

I had the luck to see the River Tidris in my teens.
Sunset pink veiled the riverside
and colored the western horizon.
Palm trees stretch high all along the shore,
elder brothers guarding their flowing brother below.

Evening winds wave the fronds, butterflies
against the vast pink background, I am excited
remembering the 1001 childhood stories
I grew up hearing. Surrounded, floating,
dazzled between east and west, past and present.

Like Zhuan Tee, the great saint and scholar,
who fancied himself a fluttering butterfly.
Time and tide no longer fencing him, he lived
in a realm beyond. Evening prayer call awakened
me to ritual reverence of the Almighty, calming

me to awareness of my smallness, as I travel
the world made by Him. I cannot finish
my awesome eternal thanksgiving.

Leila Joiner
Published in OASIS Journal

Screwdriver

The butt end of the screwdriver
bores a hole through my palm,
calloused by edges frayed by turnings
and twistings that never drive home
the crooked screw bent from so many
years mishandling.

"Make me a screwdriver," she says.
"Just one more, then I'll go home."
The bartender wipes a glass clean,
pours fake o.j., tops it off with gin and
a slice of lime – her own peculiar taste -
the glass slippery in her hand,
cold sweat rim on the the cocktail napkin.
"Ring around the rosy, " she sings
and traces the wet circle with a forefinger.

Push a screw hard enough and he'll get back
at you. That's what they tell you the first
time they lock you up, before they throw
away the key and you think there's still
a chance you can be on the outside
just like any joe. I've been screwed,
you think, but don't say out loud,
don't want to give them ideas.
You twist and turn yourself into
the quiet places, into slots and holes
no one else has filled yet, so only the nub
of you is visible to the naked eye.
Leave just enough showing so the screwdriver
can find your head and wind you out
when the time comes.

Her drink is almost gone now.
The house waits empty. The bar
will be empty soon, too. The cell
overflows with space left over
after the screws have turned in.

Larry Harmer

Mr. Grey's Cabin

A July 25, 1990 forest fire (the "Dude" fire) east of Payson, AZ, destroyed a monument to the romance of the West. Some of the stories that were born there are woven into this poem. There are 21 Zane Grey titles in this poem.

In the mountains of Arizona, near the top of the Mogollon Rim,
Stands the shell of a once proud cabin that the "Dude Fire" dun in.

It stands as a stark reminder of its past days and its glory.
A tribute to a time when Mr. Grey would pause to weave a story.

Before William S. Tom Mix or Hoot, before Hoppy, Gene or Roy,
Mr. Grey's tales brought the West alive for many a young boy.

The titles on the book backs were stories in themselves,
When as a young lad I'd stare up at Grandpa's shelves.

I'd sit <u>Under the Tonto Rim</u> and ride <u>The Rainbow Trail</u>.
I was left with little doubt that Mr. Grey could tell a tale.

<u>50,000 on the Hoof</u> and <u>Riders of the Purple Sage</u>.
My eyes grew wide in wonder as I poured over every page.

I'd chase the <u>Raiders of the Spanish Peaks</u> 'til they were down to <u>The Last Man</u>.
Then I'd follow the <u>Mysterious Rider</u> and listen to the <u>Call of the Canyon</u>.

I rode up on <u>Wild Horse Mesa</u> on my way up to <u>Thunder Mountain</u>.
And return down <u>West of the Pecos</u> like a <u>Wanderer of the Wasteland</u>.

But the "Dude Fire" raged ... and the flames ... they did prevail
And caused Mr. Grey's cabin to travel down its <u>Last Trail</u>.

Mr. Grey's cabin gave birth to strength, courage, and trust,
From the <u>Last of the Plainsmen</u> to the <u>Man of the Forest</u>.

That simple cabin is gone now and I'm heavy with sorrow
As I remember a time when I would ride the back of <u>Tappan's Burro</u>.

<u>The Hashknife Outfit</u> has suffered and a piece of our soul is lost.
<u>The Knights of the Range</u> have realized what really matters most.

<u>The Heritage of the Desert</u> has moved up those <u>Stairs of Sand</u>,
But the <u>Spirit of the Border</u> will never leave his land.

Thank you, Zane Grey.

Richard Humphries

To Some, A Life is Simply Being

To some, a life is simply being, time spent here with little meaning.
Some days are good, others bad, most somewhere between the two are clad.
Among the lucky ones am I, aware each day that when I die
My time on earth has gone as planned, with only God to make the span.
He planned the clouds and all the rain, and other things I can't explain.
Thankfully, he let me know that only He can stem the flow.
His love for me is oh so great, that never do I doubt my fate,
And smile upon my growing years, aware there is no need for tears.
My days are short, my time is near, and with His love, I have no fear.
With that in mind, I hold my wife and thank her for this joyous life.
She, far more than any other, hath caused the joy I hereby utter.
She, a love, mother, serious friend, enhanced my view to which I trend.
Daughters she has given me, both of whom have made me see
That life can have its ups and downs, replete with love that knows no bounds.
The sun sinks low behind the hill, another sign of our God's will.
I marvel at the beauty surrounding His display, and know full well He
Will repeat it, each time in His own way.

Peggy Gigstad
Published in Harmony Magazine

Monsoon Minute

A wet brick wall glows rust
like rectangular basketballs
throwing light back to the sideways sun
fiber optic birds of paradise pulse orange, yellow
even rocks are blushing
Roses move like a red velvet curtain
ready to signal the end of this show

Sometimes the sun rides on the tail of a storm into twilight
bringing the desert from muted to manic and back again
But first, one last moment of grace a fleeting final bow
a reminder just in case you didn't hear
the thunders answers each flash
with some applause or a whimper
signaling the end either way

This is another kind of light
that cannot linger
golden and gone in a monsoon minute
the air rings and colors vibrate
like a tuning fork soon silent

Dan Gilmore

First T.V.

My mother took a moral stand against it,
said television was the work of the devil,
said my father's wanting it showed how
weak he really was. But, for once, he stood
firm. It was a blond GE with a twelve inch
screen – a blond whore my mother couldn't
have hated more. After supper, we sat on the sofa

in the dark, my mother wedged in the middle,
hands over her ears, back straight, her worn
leather Bible on her lap. My father switched it on.
Roller Derby came at us like a train on fire,
women on skates trying to kill one another -
knees to the midsection, elbows to the neck,
hair pulling, eye gouging. Suddenly, my mother
leaned forward and yelled, "Kill her. Oh, kill her.
Hit her in the mouth." She jabbed us with her elbows,
moved to the edge of the sofa. Her Bible lay splayed
at her feet like an injured player. During a commercial
she read aloud from John 12:46 *I am come a light
into the world, that whosoever believeth on me
should not abide in darkness.* Amen, she said, as the men

took the track. She marked her place with a finger,
sat forward again and yelled, "Kill him, kick him.
That's it. Oh, hurt him." My father excused himself
to get a glass of water. I sat on the floor to escape
her sharp elbow. And years later, this is the way
I remember her alone, agitated, the empty space

around her expanding, the wild, festering pleasure
she took in wrestling, boxing, and roller derby, that Bible
always within reach, proof to all that a better place awaited her.

Charles Portolano

The Vastness of You

I travel far to find
such a sight as you,
a wonder of the world,
for no matter how far
I ever travel
I will never reach
the end of your love,
vast as the Grand Canyon;
your being so deep as
your river of love cuts
through the curving
canyons of my mind.
I follow after you
in your path.
I see the beginning
of our time together
that will never end
for I can only guess
how long it took
to create these walls
of your being.
Scanning up and down
your being
I find answers
to questions
only dreamed of
for you
are timeless,
as our love grows
ever deeper
cutting through
the landscape of my being…

your vastness
changes me forever.

Mark Young

There Were Promises

The streetlamp burns yellow at day's end,
reaches with light fingers into shadows,
past moths and insects flitting
against the filament in spastic rhythms.
They hum around the glow like cherubim
singing *glory, glory to you, oh bulb.*

You've been taught about this intersection -
the corner of Flaxen and Goldbrick.
Past the buzz and hum you think
you hear whispers and laughter.
One voice sounds like your grandmother.

And you expect it to be. And you expect
to see your cat Fred, your first pet,
who dies on the back porch in December
snow and your mom picked him up
with a shovel and placed him in a Converse
shoe box and then in the basement freezer.

In the spring, when the ground thawed
you and your brother buried Fred
under the cedar tree in your back yard.
You went back late one night after everyone
was in bed and sat under the tree, away
from the porch light. You asked questions.

Fred didn't answer. Neither did grandma.
And the preacher didn't seem to know,
not exactly, although there were promises.

Ona Lesa Foster

Ancient Dreams

The mountains on the horizon,
like poets, put on
purple thoughts against the
golden clamor of the day just past,
crumpling and collapsing -
exhaling the dark night.

A sighing wind is driving ancient
dreams over the dead sea,
lulling us finally,
to careworn sleep.

In our dreams, we cry ourselves so dry,
we are sifted by the wind
that in daylight burns the desert's
golden hills...

and fall lightly to the desert floor,
as if we were but blossoms
from the palo verdes,
blown off the trees by these
sighing winds.

Jay Dusard

Cactus, Sand, and Stone

There's a wretched, wretched region
Of the cactus, sand, and stone.
Where time's an endless season...
And man's spirit's free to roam.

Here... the soul is but a whisper
Floating swift across the land
Sharing secrets with saguaros
Who stand sentinel and grand.

It celebrates the barrels
Who bloom though discontent...
For they are born survivors
And stay true to their intent.

In this hot and prickly region
Of the cactus, sand, and stone
The eastern sky is warming
As a horseman rides alone.

In the coolness of the hour
He sets hoof upon the ground...
Striding long across a landscape
As far melodies resound.

The morning dove is cooing
And the gamble quail now call
To the coyote who is wailing...
At the magic of it all.

The horseman, now, is leaning
As he trots along the trail...
Watching close... and waiting...
For the signs that will not fail.

The branches that are broken...
And the imprints in the sand
Will tell the tail of cattle
Who here have taken stand.

Soon... all's quiet in the desert
And the songs of sunrise cease
No sound is heard descending
As the canyon walls increase

Now... A splash of color casting
In the shadows dark and dim
Below the beaned mesquite trees...
Underneath the canyon's rim

There... sheltered from sensations
Of a sultry, smoldering sky
Stand the horned and painted legends
Of historic tales gone by.

They are survivors of the desert
A mere mystery of the land
Whose beauty is deceptive
As the sparkling, sunlit sand.

There's a toughness to the spirit
And yet a sinew-ed grace
In these cattle of the cowboy's
That indwell this desert place.

The cowboy's found his purpose...
Where the granite spheres are shear
And the water trickles downward
Toward grasses growing near.

In this wanting, writhing region
Of the crucifixion thorn
There are souls that share a secret...
Here a kindred spirit is born.

Corrientes and the cowboy
Rooted deep in mystery lore
Share the secret of the desert
To survive... *a season more.*

Don Davison
Published in Iris and Other Things: A Collection

A Mountain Man

To make a mark on the hidden world of dreams,
I have piled earth and set stones into a mound.
From the grave there is yet a glorious link to the truth.
The form remains,
Called from beyond the now,
standing on some mist-shrouded shore of time.
Who will see the ground's swell?
If and when,
Piqued wonder will cement a truth of presence that
will say,
Who was he?
Why was he here?
What did he intend to do?
It matters not,
the mound remains,
casting a shadow in the low light of the sun's late rays.
And finally,
in passing on his way into tomorrow,
a lonely rider tips his hat to what was
and moves on towards what he hopes will be.
A solitary silhouette disappears in the midst
of momentary social intercourse.
How difficult to see,
to catch and hold,
to know how it is that justice owns each syllable of time.

Sheila Murphy

Toward a New Year

One whittles something, perhaps to reckon with an atmosphere in which the strategy remains *produce, send forth, consume*. From cold the wild geese fly away. In a pattern of advance/recede, velocity's amended. The human spirit falls to virtuosic silence. As if to shift the factual in favor of the show. Perception's inexperience informs oncoming history. Whose viscosity inverts clear thought during deliberation of a wind quintet.

A trellis poised mid-snow, hosting the myth of climb until it's so

Lisamarie Jelderks

Mistletoe

Mistletoe watches
Like spider from its web
Capturing kisses.

Lisamarie Jelderks

Winter

Snowdrops break through ice
As white crystal falls above
Nature is stirring.
My belly grows heavy now
Even winter brings new life.

Bob Atkinson

Billy

Billy had you scratching head
you'd not know what to make
of his mild and witty manner
which changed in a quick eye blink

Billy was full of wonderment
about those exciting things
is Earp really a fast draw?
or
can a dozen Apaches catch him?

many of us settle in
to a confined behavioral space
he was never boxed into
activity which him constrained

always looking for the way
pieces of a puzzle fit
caused him grief sometimes
which he saw as excitement

in those days of violent ways
in the heart of never lands
where those of different cultures
formed their cultured bands

care was given to protect
what man had carved out from
those hills and mountains so beautiful
in the land of much hot sun

others saw what had been gathered
as spoils of a strange war
between those
that had worked so hard for wealth
and those who wanted more

much was there to take in spoils
if one could run away fast
always some who saw a rope
and a tree as frontier justice

some would dance the dance of days
that had come and gone
some would dance the dance of lust
as new opportunities for thievery dawned

some would try to live within
the rules others far away made
some would push boundaries (like Billy did)
putting them into early graves

Philip Boatright

What Ken Bacher Saw From His Roof, Looking Down on the Mexican Bird of Paradise

Butterfly darting
this fast! bull's eye in orange
full on to the next.

PJ Scheidel

The Man in the Door

Title suggested by Steve Miller

I served in the white house and was very proud to do so.
And I'd like to think that there was meaning to my life.
I saw many leaders of the world come and go.
But by my side, through it all, was my wife.

She was there in the beginning when I was very young,
Just starting out, when being a black man wasn't easy.
I received both praise and slights from the friends I was among,
But my wife kept me grounded with the love that she gave me.

I served in the White House for thirty-four years,
Serving eight Presidents and many Heads of State.
I was at the top of my field amongst all my peers,
Savoring the good times and ignoring the hate.

I lived a full life and have memories I'll cherish
Of some who were famous and of many who were not.
I loved my job... for what more could anyone wish.
I hope people were pleased with the service they got.

For years, only a humble butler I may have been,
But I served my country in my own special way.
If I possibly could, I would do it all again.
There's no less pride in a job done well every day.

Debby Mitchell

Heat

middle of the road
edge of a cliff rocky
and deep the ravine
cottonwood trees
and so far away from the car

do you hear the tkkkk
rattle   disturbed   warning

it is all a warning at some point
the veins of the pink cacti blossom
curving with the breeze
so soft, so angry
bees cradled in the pollen
while flags of orange tip the ocotillo
bending in the warm air

morning
and I am lost here
somewhere in the mountains
north, north of cave creek
and looking for

the emptiness of sound
The silence of the desert
Its sharp presence
Knowing

Who can live here
Who can come through the heat

Mary S. Crume
Published in Mood Swings

Caught in a Mirage

Open range was a playground
for mavericks like Marj and me.
No billboards to blur free choice
or rail tracks to mark the wrong side.
I can still feel those silky miles -
that space between blue mesas
and our hounds breaking the silence.
Wild thermals etched bloom
from our cheeks, a worthy tradeoff,
we thought, for views not crowded
with elms or shaped by forebears.

I look at this ravaged land, ponder
what we should have seen
crouched in the shivering heat.

JoAnn Breul

I Am Love

I am love,
I am puppies,
And snowflakes,
And daffodils,
And snakes,
I am nature,
And the cosmos,
And little specks of flakes,
I am H2O and electrons
Floating in space,
I am the unseen forces
Of gravity's grace,
I am love,
Just a wave that I ride,
in sync with the tones,
That vibrate alike,
With the purest of forms,
The forces of light,
that flow through my veins,
And course with my essence,
I am shadow, and dark,
The ego so stark,
I am Neanderthal enlightened,
With bliss on my face,
I am thriving and growing
Stalks sprouting in place,
I am all that there is,
And all that there was,
I am everything
As it surges with love.

mikel weisser

Trickle (Rapidly)

The rapids are always ghostlike in photos
Like memories of all
The water washing at the bridge
In the moment -

- it's the chuckle and trilling
That lap at your attention
The fireworks display
Narrowing your focus
From depth to surface, droning off time
To its own unending tape loop
It's the sound of a song that won't remember to end

As above ferns and ivies lap themselves silly
Inhaling the vapors, indulging the humor
Of splashes like tickles ghost fingers extend
To the loves they hold close
Nestled to their hard heart below

Sparks, sparkling, and vibrantly flashing
Endlessly extending their dance of variation
Each moment an intoxicated illusion

That water knows no gravity -

- And in photographs it's only the ghosts that remain
A mere masque of the stones
A memory of water alive

Jody J. Thompson

A Quick One Near 4th Avenue

Look at you.
Leaning in,
awkward.

Sitting on a concrete bench on top of gravel.
Both feet planted firmly on
the ground.

Rolling the soles of your shoes
from right to left.
Back and forth.

This is it.

Suzanne L. Cochran

Rain

Rain!
From whence does it come?
From the breath of God upon oceans blown.
Waters travel thru the sky,
To fall on desert floor or mountains high.

Rain!
Constant need in a desert parched,
Born by clouds high and arched,
Pours down to cleanse and nourish
Dusty ground the plants to flourish.

Rain!
Heaven borne that God has sent.
Ending the deserts dry lament.
Cattle eagerly seek
New grass, tender and sweet.

Rain!
Life from the Giver sent,
To ease the desert by dryness rent,
All creatures large and small
By the rain are held enthralled.

Marge Pellegrino

The Corner of Stewart and Lawrence

In darkness
snow shrouds unseen forms

Icy fingers clenched in muffled silence
ache for a warm caress

Where dogwood once reached for sky
Emptiness

Another tree planted in Spring
will never fill the heart space

C. J. Wright

The Surf

the surf
the white froth of the giant waves spilling onto the black
black lava shore looking so angry
as the line breaks down the rugged coast
the black crabs scurrying to hold on in the swirls
each wave threatening to be the great one that breaks over the sea
wall
the tide pools for just a moment spilling small falls over
its lava basin till the incoming wave fills it again
the promise of a sunset, yet another disappointment
as the distant fog bank keeps the green flash hidden until another
day
the deep healing of the soul that will remember
this time 1,000 years from now
a family an ohana has come together
to laugh play and grow the love deeper with memories for another
time.

Hazel Ray

Legacy

From Dorothy, Dorwan and Phyllis:
Role models for us all
On a life well lived.
Will someone ever say of me
What has been said of them?
Thank you, dear friends,
For showing me
That my being here
Can make a difference to
Countless others

From John:
True justice abides
In the heart
As well as the mind.
Can I learn to exercise
Righteous judgment?
Thank you, your Honor,
For reminding me to see others
As they truly are
And not through a smoke screen
In my mind.
From Gabe:
A sudden change
In the course of life
Can I transform
To meet the unexpected
With grace and poise?
Thank you, Gabe,
For strengthening my faith
That in God's Greater Plan
There is always a place for me.

From Christina:
A bundle of potential
Bursting to express.
Can I bring forth
My unique combination
Of talents and skills
With such joy and love?
Thank you, Christina,
For the nurturing spirit
You have engendered
At the dawn of a new era
For humankind.

To all, I hold you in the light
And give thanks for this legacy.

Mark Bahti

There Was a Time When Poems Had Power

There was a time when poems had power.
Not the power to stir imaginations,
to evoke images,
but power.
Not the power to move men
but the power to make men move.
When the pause between words
made people hold their breath,
transformed by what had been said,
and afraid of what would follow.

Words built the world, they were our instructions.
Poems told our history, they kept it alive for each generation
and formed the future, calling out where we were to go
and how to get there.

Poems did not merely say,
they foretold.
And they retold, weaving what once was into a narrative of what
would be
weaving our future out of our past.

There was a time when poems had power.
Real power.
True power.
They had to be spoken carefully -
thoughtfully -
knowing what they could create.
The turn of a word could mean
life or death,
peace or war.

Immense power spoke through poems
each word a footfall,
each pause a gathering of strength,
a gathering of clouds,
as if drawing breath before moving forward.

Yes,
there was a time when poems had power.
And we stood,
waiting for the power of words to rain down upon us.

Maria Rodriquez-Pope

Today

Today I see short men only
They come
They go
Some of them walk slowly
Pounding the earth
Searching for the stones
Of growth
Others swing from side to side
Music inside
Chanting nostalgia
Remembering sweet wine
Childlike, chocolate mind
Others walk spaced out
Touching the air
With their pupils
Refusing to cry
Green mirrors of tears
Hidden
Today I only see short men
Finding their visions
Flowers in their hands
Pain flowing away
Short men reaching for the sky

Regina Nelms

Coyote Crucifix

near my home I watch
an artificial, tinseled tree
rush by on monsoon waters.

Indian Bend Wash purges
Arizona's high desert of once functional objects –
tires, bikes, bones and broken fences surge past.

and then I see him.
tangled in an uprooted palo verde branch,
arms splayed and forehead bound by barbed wire,
he struggles, impaled – a floating, fur crucifix.

I run alongside.
so close the river drenches me – a deluge of holy water.
he seems to know I can't save him.
I am forgiven…washed clean.

then as if on the back of
a golden, liquid whale,
he rises up, and slips downstream.

I wonder if it is his progeny
who ate the neighbor's cat during the blood moon,
then danced in the dry wash, and
growled with delight .

celebration of an ancient rite –
the coyote howl.

Jen Reich

Be

Feel the sun
Even if it's dark
Talk to birds
Play in the park
Hug a tree
Or bust a move
Let your spirit feel the groove -
For each moment is our only chance
To touch the magic of our dance -
And if we live for now not then
We'll know that when our time is through
We learned to be
As well as do~

Jim Tayburn

A Heavenly Vision

Twas the night before Christmas; all the hoopla turned down
It was quiet as a mouse all over town
Shopping done, stockings, hung, end of the rush
In every corner of the house, a welcome hush

We were all tucked away, snug in our beds
Christmas morning visions danced in our heads
Suddenly, there appeared a penetrating light
So overwhelming, it extinguished the night

I leapt out of bed, in a complete dither
Not knowing where to run, yon or hither
Just as my choice was about to be made
There came this voice, "Don't be afraid"

The apparition was shimmering and oh so bright
Shielding my eyes, I shivered in fright
My heart was racing, my blood pressure high
Then again the voice, "It is I"

"It is I, the first and the last
Not the ghost of Christmas future or Christmas past
I who knew you before you were born
Have been with you since the curtain was torn"

"It's okay, the Santa Claus myth
but I'm here to offer you the ultimate gift
The one for which He suffered at Calvary
In payment of our sins for all eternity"

As He spoke, a quiet peace settled on my soul
I accepted His gracious gift and re-born role
There were changes coming in my behavior
And I would teach my children of our Lord and Savior

I awoke to pitter patter and a child's scream
But this experience was more than just a dream
Santa Claus would continue to visit our place
But we'd also make room for His amazing grace

Church would no longer be just an obligation
There'd be time for prayer and celebration
I had accepted the Holy Spirit's call
It truly would be a Merry Christmas for all.

Stuart Watkins

A Tribute to Little Robe

Little Robe,
Son of Geronimo, Apache Chief,
Age 2 Years, 1885
So few words to tell of the life and death of a two year old boy.
Did he die in his mother's arms?
Was Geronimo off raiding a Mexican village?
Did the boy suffer?
Why was he buried in the Fort Bowie cemetery?
Did muffled drums beat slowly as he was lowered into the grave?
Who was there?
Little Robe, Son of Geronimo, Apache Chief,
Age 2 Years, 1885.
(Goyahkla was Geronimo's real name.)

Stuart Watkins

Time on Their Hands

Retired persons all have Time on their Hands.
They wait for a phone call from their sons, daughters,
or other loved ones.
They bike, run, play bridge, and golf,
still, they all have Time on their Hands.
The call they anticipate comes,
or comes not,
but they wait.
Retired persons know their children
have lives of their own,
but still…
Call, please call, because all they have is
Time on their Hands.
"Oh, hello? Mom, is that you?"
"Yes, dear, thanks for calling."

Jonathan Messenger

When the Purple Shadows Fall

The shadows of the evening cross this lonely trail,
    As I rein my pony toward the home corral,
His head is hangin' low, and my weary heart is yearnin',
    To be rockin' on the front porch with my gal.
We should be ridin' easy, as we rock along for home…
    But I'm thinkin' as the purple shadows fall…
That if the highways and the houses keep creepin' 'cross the range,
    That soon there won't be nothin' left at all.

We're ridin' tighter circles on an ever shrinkin' range…
    And the leases that we're payin' take a bigger piece of change…
And the ghosts of empty saddles never seemed so real at all…
    As they do now, when the purple shadows fall.

When the old men rode these mountains, all the range was wild and free,
    In the days before the spoilin' of the land…
Come the wire, then the concrete, they began to tear apart,
    A way of life they refused to understand.
Now they say it needs protectin', this blessed range of ours…
    An' they're claiming that the cattle are to blame…
As the asphalt stain of progress creeps like cancer 'cross our range,
    An' this life we love may never be the same.

And the voices of the old hands seem to whisper in my ear,
    That the time to make a change is drawing near…
As they spur their ponies through the clouds you can hear their ghostly call…
    Come lately, when the purple shadows fall.

Now I'm thinkin' 'bout my children, as the homestead comes in view,
    In the distance I can hear the cattle bawl…
Is there justice for a cowman in this troubled land of ours,
    Do these children have a future here at all?
Don't bite the hand that feeds you… that's what my grandpa said…
    His words of wisdom I can still recall…
Lord, these folks that we've been dealing with don't seem to understand,
    That they've got us with our backs against the wall.

The time has come to stand and fight, that's what the old men say...
    If you listen, you can hear 'em ask us all...
Which side will you be choosin'... when the Judgment Riders call,
    Some evenin'... when the Purple Shadows fall... ?

Oh, which side will *you be choosin'*... when the Judgment Riders call,
    Some evenin'...
        When the Purple Shadows fall...

Heather Ackerman

Translucency

I feel translucent.
People can see me, but I grow cloudier with each day that goes by.
I was a clear image in the beginning.
But, as time goes on, I have become harder to see.
Tears, pain, time, and new memories all make me harder to remember.
But, there is one thing; no matter how many tears are shed,
no matter how much pain there is, no matter how much time goes by,
and no matter how many memories flood minds of those who were there,
they will never forget the night of the accident.
The crash, the glass, the people dying, and people crying
are all still memories that haunt
each and every person at the scene.
The driver was dead, and his passengers, too.
I didn't make the decision they did,
but I am paying for their bad judgment.
They gave in; I did not.
They are dead now, and so am I.
Why do I have to pay; why do I have to die?
This is not fair for me; it is not fair for my family.
Now, as each day goes by, and I'm not there with them,
I will become harder to remember.
I sit here now with no other way to describe –
the only thing I feel is translucent inside.

Don Davison

Thunderhead

(Over the San Francisco Peaks)

The blackening gray cloud cap sits gently
on the head of the mountain
and shrouds its shoulder with its breath.
Infinitesimal droplets finally condense to mist –
Congealed Sacred Tears
falling upon the needles of the alpine apron
of the peaks.
Then, gently do they slide off boughs,
crashing down to the fronds of the bracken
just before they shatter on the ground –
again, fragments of His breath.
They flow into one
enveloping the whole in a mantle of Silver Life.
Eventually,
sinking and flowing through crevices
around bits of molten moments,
at last they arrive.
Slipping through silten remains
they lend a softness to their journey
and finally occupy that pregnant synapse,
laying their gifts at the tips of the rhizomes.
And slowly then they sacrifice
their aggregated integrity,
their dipole wholeness,
as they break apart.
In Miguel Angelo fashion,
the Tip of the Finger of the Father
touches soul into life.

Agnes Paulsen

Immigrants

A century ago,
    my mother was nine
    my dad was twelve
    living in Denmark
    miles apart
    not knowing each other

there were no
    radios
    cars
    T.V.s
    microwaves
    computers

you might say people lived a simple life
    or was it simple?

people fought with each other
    in private and in public
    made peace
    forgave and forgot

they played games
    talked
    sang
    worked in the fields

had dreams
    like my mother
        who wanted to come
        to America
        to be a missionary
    like my dad
        who was looking for a new life
        in America

rumors had it that the streets in America were paved with gold
    so when my dad was eighteen

        he sailed for America
        went to live with Danish relatives in Michigan
        caned chairs for a living
        saved money for an education
when my mother was twenty
        she immigrated to America
        the land of her dreams
        went to live with a missionary acquaintance
        in Chicago
        found work in a sewing factory

The new millennium of 2000 is on the horizon
        one of my grandchildren is nine
        another is twelve

I have a
        radio
        car
        T.V.
        microwave
        computer

my parent's dream of a better life is mine

but life in this world is not simple

people continue to fight with each other
        in private and in public
        sign peace treaties
        break them
        compete for power

new immigrants come to America
        sew clothes in sweat shops
        harvest crops
        clean the homes of the wealthy

and dream of a better life
        for their children.

Lyle Paulsen

The Soft Fingers of Twilight

The soft fingers of twilight
      have come to massage my soul.
The golden rays of the setting sun
      with warm soothing strokes
      caress the rhythms of my mind
      to a calmness of quiet peace.
The birds are settling in for the night
      and know too the natural need
      to rest from their quest of nourishment,
      for the morrow will surely come again.
The sun is not really going down.
And with a simple perspective switch
      I can almost sense the shadows moving
      as the earth turns its face to the west
      and another day is measured
      on the cosmic calendar of time.
How reassuring it is to be in sync
      with such unchangeable rhythms.
And yet how utterly fascinating to behold
      the colors turn and soften and deepen
      as their hues mix on the evening pallet.
How awesome are the golden rays
      that climb the mountains and then the clouds
      reflecting the stuff that fills the atmosphere.
The stars too distant to compete with the sun
      now can come into my growing awareness
      with new pristine and sparkling clarity.
And my soul takes on the immensity
      of this vast and amazing universe.

Harvey Bornfield

For My Beautiful Wife Gail

Your children are vibrant, inquisitive, devoted, vulnerable yet confident. You have raised them with care. They have captured this and will carry forth this most valuable of powers, this most precious of legacies into the world at large. In so doing, they will continue to civilize us all with light.

I have been able to see the children and interact with them for the first time in years. So, I am going to throw away all my crippled songs and learn some new ones – ones a person can carry into battle as well as hum in a quiet garden. To be inspired and fragile is to go through life distracted. You can't acquire peace of mind much less wisdom by allowing beauty and trauma to hold sway over the moment, by victimizing yourself with such give and overwhelm as rupture one's resolve to act.

So, another power is needed. This time spent apart provides an opportunity to trade in a prayer and a sword for a good pair of shoes. The horizon is the way of seeing the whole picture, of many things blurred into one whole at a great distance. But, when these approach and assume details as every responsibility at hand requires, the telescope of the stargazer must be put away, or at least saved for the unborn future. The future it was meant to track, approaching over the horizon of the distant sea of all things coming.

I will sharpen my tools and expect to use them, break them, and repair them. Meanwhile, I will teach the children that one does not clean up rooms, or fix coolers, or set alarm clocks with staples from eternity. Although, they do help to bolster us – allowing our acts to glide when they might otherwise hobble.

I hope you have taken in a fair share of wonder and awe, and allowed yourself the great gift of being impressionable to the art all around you, the handiwork of another culture that should offer a mysterious and colorful contrast to our own. It's time to cultivate a few grapes, to work in the vineyard and to trust that God knows enough chemistry and alchemy to keep the affairs of the human race well directed.

Michael Cochran

Again and Again

The day is ending as the sun settles gratefully to rest,
While colors of purple, lavender, and rose form slowly in the west.
Gone the sounds of voices many, each scrambling, a frantic quest.
Now stillness waits in silent hush as night approaches, a welcome guest.

The sleeper lies with eyes of peace uncaring in a dreamless state,
But we are loathe to mark the ending of one more hour, though late.
So on we walk with cat-like steps, our breath withheld in silent care,
As thru the night we move together into a realm few ever dare.

Slow as the night does nestle in, our hearts unwind, beginning to blend;
From peace without that flows within to ease our burden, each soul to mend.
Then all is still and pausing in place, we hold each other and silently wait,
As darkness fills a mysterious hush when night rises up to meet her fate.

With sudden abandon a voice lashes forth in joyous delight of rippling song,
Whose ending repeats again and again from cliff-side and valley ever so long
Again it's repeated in just the same way filling the night from o'er the hill,
As from afar the notes filter in of the joyous song of the whip-poor-will.

We stand unmoving, not daring to break the silence that follows the song in its wake.
Then ever so soft, just barely we hear a final answer, our souls to sear.
At last our senses return with a rush; night breezes whisper, sent from above,
Shedding the hold of mysterious night, we move toward home in the arms of love.

Taba Dale

Lone Flier

The summer sun is rising,
higher and higher

I hear the drone of a plane,
it's a lone flier

A little lizard slithers
seeking bugs or some shade

While cactus wrens dive
for a nest they have made

Quirky quail dither and run,
zig-zagging to rejoin their brood

There goes a frisky jackrabbit
it has prey to allude

Another stands under a bush,
still as a statue

Don't worry my friend,
I won't hurt you

Is that a feathered spirit
atop the granite outcropping?

Could it be the Harris Hawk?
He's watching. Not talking.

There goes another plane
somewhere up high

Way above the mountaintops
jutting into blue sky

The heat bothers not
the dancing butterfly

Alas, I turn home
and to the desert, say goodbye.

Alana Helapitage

Mother

She has watched me,
With a daybreak light in her hazel eye

She has hummed with her lips pursed to my little head
Made my pulse and breath
By the murmur and scent of her kisses

She is my clarity.
She is my home.

But I am a woman, now… ?

Ripped from my swaddling blankets
And my fetal sleep
Time has somehow given me to the world
I am small, young… yes

Still I want to meander in the cold draught, now

I am a woman, now…

In the light of my heart, swollen as a heavy rose and ripped:

Bleary-eyed,
My sight is still my clarity

Shaking,
My home is still my own nakedness

Slack-jawed,
My word is still my God.

I am a woman, now.

God, how did I grow prostrate and lithe?
How do I even walk?

Animate by grace I hold as heartily
As I could ever hold to *Her*

Both blaze and blade,
I will charge, and cut my chains
I will watch over myself
Through dark, and light.

I am a woman, now.

James E. Cox

The Moth

The moth seeks the flame.
For Man it is love's vague game…
both tempt destruction

James E. Cox

'Tis Time

'Tis time, indeed, that you appraise
the misspent hours within Life's maze
there are never enough tomorrows
to amend lost yesterdays.

James E. Cox

Hubris

Those tales that from the ages pass
rather than teach, create morass.
The winner narrates with hubris cast;
the loser's scorn makes gold look brass.

Marilou Schunter
Guest Poet from Culpeper, VA

Mascara

Illuminize, volumize, millionize your eyes!

bearded scallop shell eyes
a powerful tool in the pursuit of love
curved black tentacles
spring open, clamp shut

shiny, wavy lashes move in unison
hinged to iridescent glitter lids
like sleek black-stockinged Rockettes,
lift, lower, lift, lower
come on over

Want "world at your feet" eyelashes?

Apply malachite, charcoal, paraffin,
guanine extracted from fish scales
then lay in wait, to catch… a fish
and the world is full of so many.
We are fishers of men!

We curl, define, extend, thicken, darken
test the limits of neotery –
large eyes associated with innocence
like martyrs

eyelash sacrifice for the good of the whole
permanent change lashtastic
side effects may cause lids to turn black –
but eyelash allure is paramount

for most mortals, the job of the eyelash
is to keep dust out of the eye

striped colored lids,
edged with razor-sharp bowed black lines,
thorny lionfish fins, delicate
but deceptively poisonous,
ultimately compelling

lashes glide open, shut
venetian blinds
on hotel windows

amazing mascara will
attract a husband, stop traffic,
lengthen my legs,
bring fame and fortune –
those are some powerful eyelashes!

Maybelline – you saved my life!

Bonita Blankenship
Dedicated to Carol Raney

Yes, I've Seen a Javelina

Yes, I've seen a javelina
They're not fat, nor are they leana
You could say they're just right
For a peccary their width and height

They still eat the neighbor's cactus
We've watched them munch our own hibiscus
They're omnivorous, come one, come all
Down the gullet, they have a ball

As to their odor, it's kinda skunky
The smell exceeds an unwashed monkey
Their scent glands keep them close together
It can outlast any weather

They watch their young with careful eye
Keep them close, so don't try
To snatch the pig-like young
You might feel like you'd been stung

So, I like the javelina
I think they're all kinda keen-a

Erdeen Evertsen

Friendship's Rose

I often think in rhyming verse,
And 'ere my time is spent
I sit alone and paint a rose
To pay a compliment.

For there are many whom I love
To whom I never tell
The gratitude that's in my heart
For the things they do so well.

It seems we easily forget
That bit of praise to say
When we are busy or disturbed
With the burdens of the day.

Oh, if we knew how they await
That bit of praise to hear,
We'd paint more roses for our friends
And then be more sincere.

Helen Spencer Schlie

The World Has Charms

The world has charms that magnetize my heart
To dream of lands and seas, of leaves and trees
To stand against the winds off Barbary Coast
To shade my eyes against the gleam of sun
    On Kilimanjaro's snow-frosted peaks
To feel the sting of sands blown off Sahara's dunes
    Where camels fret their long lashed eyelids
    As camels have for eons past
To glide through blue-green waters, crystal clear
    As rainbow fishes dart in languid seaweed safety.
Yes. Let me dream
But let me be in Arizona in the Spring
    At one with Arizona in the Spring
To watch the glory in the light at dawn
    With lupine's blue dropped down from out the sky
As palo verde's golden branches pulsate
    In illuminated sun
Sunshine yellow brittle-bush adorn both crag and rocky spire
And cactus blossoms inspire
    Designs for ballet dancers' skirts
Mallow's orange reflects the setting sun
As long-nosed bats, unseen.
    Fly up from Mexico by night
    To sip the nectar of saguaro's waxy blooms
All the wonders of the earth … rest
And Arizona … sleeps.

Simmons B. Buntin
Published in Freshwater

Arc

If there is an art
to scaling desert
boulders in bare feet
it is this: my daughter,
eleven, tosses her sandals
to prickly pear
and mesquite, pries
knee into crevice,
and presses onto the sun-
drunk surface
like a lizard revealed,
hair blazing
in late afternoon
light, pants hitched
mid-calf, a hard

look of fear
and determination
before fingers and feet
release to the flat
wind, time slowed
by her sudden
leap to sharp granite
and the improbable
landing, only a thin
necklace of blood
on her ankle, red
like the thorn-guarded
flower, the arc
of a girl's first desire.

J. P. Ellsworth
Published in the Straight Scoop

The Story of C. C. Hall

The story I will tell,
Is one of C. C. Hall.
It started here in Prescott,
And, yes, I'll tell it all.

Chance Cob-web was the finest
Of late 1800's bars.
Located there on Whiskey Row,
Where patrons came from far.

The "Prop" was Capt'n Fisher,
An old sea captain staid.
'Spent years before the mast
On Pacific merchants, so t'was said.

A man of foreign ports was he.
He knew the bounding main.
The best was none too good for him
And so prosperous clients came.

One cold and wintery night,
A group had gathered for occasion,
In the Chance Saloon to warm
With spirits and pleasant conversation.

On hand this night
And of renown,
Was Col. Groom,
Who'd surveyed the town.

Besides these two were
Judge Charles Hall and Col. Bigalow,
A member of the legislature,
As everyone there did know.

Enjoying the company of all,
A Capt'n Thomas from the Fort,
And also Edmond Wells,
As his Argonaut Tales report.

As the evening wore on,
And patrons left to brave night air,
The Col. noted a bundle
At the far end of the bar.

Capt'n Fisher retrieved it
And on opening it up,
There in a wicker basket – no,
It weren't no pup.

It was a chubby, black-eyed girl,
Wrapped in a downy gown.
Both fists were fiercely sucked on.
Her thirst then knew no bounds.

Beside her there, a bottle of milk
To quench her building hunger.
As quick as any cared to think,
They all wanted her, a wonder!

They decided on a pool.
Ten dollars for a throw.
The money was a dowry,
For the baby, don't you know.

Col. Groom a bachelor,
He threw four 5's. A win?
"Hold on!" said Hall.
"I have the last throw in."

Judge Hall stood back
And shook the box hard,
He gave a mighty throw,
And four 6's his reward.

Col. Groom, now disappointed,
He claimed the right to name,
And in this most unlikely place
A Christening became.

The name he chose to call the waif
Was on the outside wall.
With glasses raised and cheers around,
He called her Chance Cobweb Hall.

The judge now headed home
To show his charming wife.
She first thot' the child was his,
But with his story saw the light.

This could have been the end
Of a story of the west,
But the travels of Edmund Wells
Gave it a different twist.

Some twenty years had passed
Since that special night.
Wells was in 'Frisco then
For business and the sights.

In the lobby of the Palace
He noted a striking pair.
Then happ'ed to hear a word or two
That made him almost stare.

This charming girl with dark, dark eyes
And very lovely face,
Had he seen her once before,
If so, where, and in what place?

The name of Prescott was what he heard,
And asked if it were home?
"Why, yes, I did grow up there and
My husband has business in Jerome."

"My father is Judge Charles Hall.
Perhaps you know of him?"
"Oh, yes. He had a daughter.
What would your name be then?"

"My name is rather strange.
I'm called Chance Cobweb Hall,
And when I would ask about it,
Dad would only smile, that's all."

So now you know the story
Of one Miss C. C. Hall.
The old west wasn't always wild,
And sometimes not at all!

Jim Hogan

The Night New Orleans Drowned

All my life I've been working
Hardly made ends meet
Never sure for certain
I could pay my rent or eat
But with double jobs
And the grace of God
I finally found the means
To buy my wife and children
A tiny home in New Orleans

Music from *The Quarter*
Would drift on down our way
Never thought a time would come
There'd be no one there to play
But when Lady K blew into town
And silenced those sweet sounds
We were roof-top wet and left for dead
The Night New Orleans Drowned

We had nowhere to go
And no way to there
When the wind started howling
On Lake Pontchartrain
Now my whole family's scattered
My house sunk and shattered
But I'm walkin' 'cross the delta
To New Orleans again

Some call her the Big Easy
But life there's filled with pain
It's the jazz and blues that eases
All the poor man's stress and strain
So the day will dawn
When we'll hear a horn
Blowin' re-birth to our town
And for a while we might forget
The Night New Orleans Drowned

Jim Hogan

Summertime In Tucson

Summertime in Tucson
Got just my cowboy boots on
'Cause in the shade it's 105
But there's no humidity
So if feels like 103
Boy I'm glad the air is dry
If you're standing real still
And factor in the wind chill
Then it's 'bout a balmy 99
So locked up inside where I reside
We can barely just survive
By crankin' down the thermostat to 65

Live in my air-conditioned house
Love my air-conditioned spouse
Feed my air-conditioned dog
While the cat is chasin'
The air-conditioned mouse.
Drive my air-conditioned kids
To their air-conditioned school
And later after workin'
When the mercury is perkin'
We venture out and
Jump into the swimmin' pool

Do you want to hear a good joke?
The devil, he got heat stroke
It's hotter here than where he's from
Don't you know God's best creation
Is cool refrigeration
It's really how the west was won

So from June until September
There's one thing to remember
'Bout living in the Old Pueblo
Come December you'll be glad
You spent the summer barely clad
It sure beats shoveling snow

When the snowbird in-migration
Has boomed the population
And the traffic's at a stop and go
It'll sure as heck beat shoveling snow

Cassius Sargent

Dry Heat

When heat exceeds the century mark
Right after end of March,
It means hot weather in the park
Will wilt a lot of starch.

When April's hot, it's certain that
May follows close behind
Plus four more months to melt your hat,
And really blow your mind.

No pearly gates adorn the town
Beneath the Tucson Sun.
Friends, I don't want to get you down,
But Summer has begun.

Archie Hoagland
Published in The Collection

Desert Sunrise

The sharp edge of the morning sun on the horizon broke,
sending its rays to drink the dew, from each leaf of the oak.
From every petal of the rose, upon the vine dew drenched,
to partake of that sweet nectar, until its thirst was quenched.

Drifting air currents formed a breeze that flowed across the land,
to mingle with the juniper, to dance across the sand.
To twist into a dust devil, to hop scotch here and there
and then dissolve to nothingness, in quiet summer air.

Each bloom shall feel the honey bee taste freely of its love.
Against the sun the red tailed hawk circles the sky above.
Coyote awaits in shady wash, the unsuspecting hare,
the piney scent of juniper perfumes the desert air.

The temperature begins to rise in step with rising sun.
Hangs half way to its zenith now upon its morning run.
The desert wears the sultry heat as woman wears a gown.
High desert after the sunrise, with morning going down.

Bonita Papenfuss

This Season

It's so dark here--this place in my mind.
There seems no release from these thoughts of dread.
A coldness envelops my very being,
and I'm despondent and fearful of the future.
I watched, with awe, for months
as he labored over her deteriorating shell,
caring for her with a deep love and commitment
borne of decades of mutual spousal devotion.
Now she's gone.
Murdered by a sinister disease
that crawled through her body
and destroyed one organ after another.
What does this season of life hold for me?
Will I remain in good health
or fall prey to disease or deformity?
Will my mind remain sharp
or will I be left stranded within its vortex
with no remembrance of my identity,
what I did with my days on this earth,
or the names of loved ones who might
gather 'round me with their faces of pity.
This time I have on earth is a gift.
I must savor every morsel that touches my lips,
etch every loving embrace onto my heart,
and live to the utmost every moment of my existence.
And I can only pray that the journey
the Good Lord chooses for my demise
might be one I'm able to navigate with dignity
and the comforting knowledge
that the darkness of my last hours
will be forever lost to the eternal glow of heaven.

Barbara Scheidel

TIME TO REFLECT AND REDIRECT

New Year's seems to me a time for introspection,
time to review the year ending, to think
of both the happy and the sad of it,
to remember the good of it and dismiss the bad of it,
to see if any actions I've taken, words I've
spoken, need mending,
and to tuck away some memories for later deeper reflection.

As this year comes to a close, I go over in my mind
acquaintances and friends I saw, people I met, the places I went.
I marvel at how quickly time flies and
wish I could say that I spent
every day just as I planned to, making a difference,
doing the task at hand
and every morning being loving, wise, compassionate and kind.

But I can't – and maybe that's the point of the New Year:
It affords us each a chance to begin our journey once more,
to decide the direction we'll take and the goals we'll strive for.
Every New Year we can regroup, re-commit to
what we're working towards,
a chance to recharge, and continue on our path without fear.

So as this year closes and another is about to start,
I wish for each of you that this coming year will impart
to you the achievement of at least one dream dear to your heart.
What better wish for the New Year could there possibly be
than to have a dream or goal we nurture become reality?

May Peace, Joy and Accomplishment
be Yours this Coming Year!

Elizabeth Doyle Solomon
Guest Poet from Barboursville, VA

New Ears for Virginia

Ninety-three year old fingers
stiff and bent with arthritis
traveled along the curvatures
of her brand new hearing aids
while I explained, loudly as
she needed, what tiny buttons
she would feel for off and on.
Eyes blinded by hard work and time
could not see these small miracles
that would be her ears, enable
her to hear many voices, birds, and
cats meowing. When she finally
fitted them into each ear, her
smile said it all. "I can hear!"
"I want to call my son," she said,
"and tell him what he's done."
From a little farm in the mountains
of Virginia, I dialed his number
in Tucson, Arizona, a world away.
"Elizabeth helped me with these
things; they are just wonderful!"
Yes, Virginia there are new ears
at ninety-three! There were tears
on her wrinkled cheeks as we prayed,
our small circle of six hands in
a land where generosity is as much
a part of this America as democracy.
Thank you, Lion's Club of Tucson!

Elizabeth Doyle Solomon is a neighbor of Virginia Hatchett Watkins (Stuart's mother) in Barboursville, Virginia.
She is the author of The Steering Wheel Poems and has written over 100,000 poems.

Joseph Harris

Poems: What They Mean To Me

Poems, you talk to me when I'm all alone,
You understand me, give support to my bones.
You offer forgiveness for transgressions
I, with other homo-sapiens, indulge,
Our aneurysms stretched to an extreme bulge.

Poems, you become a map when I'm lost,
Guideposts, through the maze of life, to home.
Making up for my mindless neglect,
Saving me from that vast silence of death,
With songs of words, the mourning blues.
Poems, you give a presence to me for those I have lost.
You make certain to raise my curtain of neglect,
You save me from my forgetfulness.
You give voice to what I do not say, but feel.

Poems, you are what makes my day,
You weave stories, catch up with my dreams,
Make it all what it seems.
You mold me, free me of grief, guilt,
Fear, or failure as I face the mirror,
Accept what I've seen,
You make me see truth, realize the beauty of life.

Poems, that is what you mean to me!

Bob Temple

The Bronc Rider

I rode out of town not very far,
Came to the gate of the old Two-Bar.
I saw a big man, looked like the boss,
Rode up to him and got off my hoss.
Told him my name, I needed a job,
"If you can ride broncs, you've got one, Bob"
"A bronc rider, I don't claim to be,
But I'll give her a try, if you agree."

That was a mistake, I'll tell you now,
I should 'a stuck to herdin' cows.
The next day I looked over them broncs,
I shouldn't have left that honky-tonk!
They were wild and ugly, lots of hair,
Eight big geldings and one little mare.
I singled out the mare, threw my rope,
If I could break her, I had some hope.

To the center post, I snubbed her tight,
She was shakin' but had lots 'a fight.
She was small and looked easy to ride,
But those squinty eyes had a certain pride.
She let me know right from the start,
This little gal had lots of heart.
I got on her and said, "Let's have her,"
I tightened my grip, the rest's a blur!

She kind 'a humped up, shook some more,
She exploded, blasted off with a roar.
She turned in mid-air, hit the ground hard,
She was smart, she caught me off guard.
My feet swung back, my head hit her neck,
I lost a stirrup, headin' for a wreck.
Back on the cantle up on the swells,
I hit the ground, laid there for a spell.

I picked myself up, looked for the mare,
From the corner, she gave me a stare.
One more time I gave it a fair try,
And one more time she made me fly.
After five tries, I finally did ride,
But not before that mare had my hide.
She wasn't very easy to break,
But in that filly, I had a stake.

Since that mare, I've broke quite a few,
On every one you learn something new.
At the Two-Bar, I earned a reputation,
I rode broncs in many a situation.
I broke some easy, lots of bad ones,
It was always work, never much fun.
As a bronc rider I was pretty fair,
My fame I owe to that little mare.

Luis Albert Yucupicio

I Am

I am from the Yoeme language and native lands
From majestic soaring eagles and beautiful red flowers
I am from burning fires and running wolves
Hunting and howling in the moonlit night

I am from deer dancers and pascola masks
From dragon scorching flames and sharp tiger claws
I am from music, art, and poetry
Where I can express myself

I am from surgery scars and chemo sickness
From M.R.I. scans, daily pills and needle points
From painful heart aches and distress
I am from a place you never want to know

But I am also from redemption and accomplishment
I am from heaven and angels in flight
Protecting, healing, and watching over me
From honest friends and loving families
I am from a world where I never feel alone
I am happy, I am strong, I am unbreakable

Richard Humphries

Southwest Soliloquy by a Bard on the Border

To fence, or not to fence, that is the question.
Whether 'tis nobler in the mind to suffer
The irreversible damage done to our realm resulting
From hordes of illegal trespassers,
Or to take arms against this
Invasion of "Willing Workers" who thumb
Their noses at our laws while crossing into Arizona.
That is the real dilemma facing America.
Should we continue to sleep, perchance to dream?
My dream is of a sovereign nation rooted in Christianity
And based upon the rule of law derived from our original Settlers.
My nightmare is of our nation becoming a borderless land
Teeming with millions of third-world invaders, welcomed
Here by a multitude of elected "leaders" residing in our
       Hall of Congress.
'Twould be far better to heed the words of the few visionaries
In power who care about the future of this great nation
Than to continue on this path of insane destruction.
Ergo… To fence, or not to fence?
If 'tis necessary to fence to cease this insanity, so be it.
Whatever it takes.

Robert A. Frost

THE LAST GUNFIGHT

This true story was told to me by the town Mayor.
Some of the actual facts are fiction, I have to be fair.

It seems an argument broke out at the Lulu Bell saloon.
The yelling got loud and everyone cleared the room.

It seems a farm hand by the name of Ben had lost his temper
Over the neighbor's wife and the money he had lent her.

Well, Marcus Mallory wasn't going to stand for any of that talk
About then the bartender stepped in and suggested each take a walk.

The dust had settled for that day, but the feud wasn't over.
Mallory couldn't step back and still keep his wife's favor.

He sent a note through Elmer Holvek challenging him to a duel.
Ben sent back a note with the picture of the back end of a mule.

It had been many years since anyone had seen an argument like this.
The usual way to settle things at that time was to use your fists.

Dueling was a popular way for gentlemen to settle arguments at one time
However, the practice lost favor, but it still wasn't a crime.

The date and time had been set and weapon would be a Colt .45.
Honor would be settled in the streets when one man left alive.

The time had arrived. It was three o'clock on Main Street.
A crowd had gathered in the shade to stay out of the heat.

Ben and Marcus stood back to back, guns raised and pale faces.
Elmer counted as each man took a step to the pre-set thirteen paces.

They turned and within three seconds four shots had been fired.
Marcus fell to his knees, mentally and physically tired.

Twenty-six paces away Ben laid still with blood coming out of his head.
The feud was settled and one good man now lay dead.

The event stirred up a lot of news and scandal at the time.
So, that's when the government made dueling in the U.S. a crime.

It's nothing to brag about and in the town there's nary a sign.
But the last gunfight in the U.S. happened in Scottsdale in 1949.

Killian Kidrick

To the Coyote, Wild and Free

We crossed paths tonight
as the gathering dusk coiled to spring night
upon us.

I wore scuffed Merrells and red polar fleece.
You wore a splendid sable coat,
and a tireless gait.

At the sight of me,
you recoiled away in subdued alarm.

Can't blame you,
me; your first and lifelong enemy.

As the earth rotated steadily upon its axis,
obliquing the sun's warning rays,
the pines creaked and moaned
in the westerly wind;
the beauty of you made me cry.

Wild and free, splendid, glorious,
you were skimming along tirelessly.

I was plodding, and burdened.

Mark Adams

Joy and Bliss

This reading is being done in prose and poetry, take your pick.

Joy is to experience great pleasure or delight. Bliss is complete paradise or heaven.

Eating pizza----Joy. Eating pizza with mushrooms and sausage----Bliss.

A medium rare steak----Joy. A medium rare Porterhouse steak----Bliss.

Boiled or baked lobster----Joy. Lobster Cantonese----Bliss.

Chocolate ice cream----Joy. Double chocolate ice cream----Bliss.

The sight of Niagara Falls----Joy. Sunset at the Grand Canyon----Bliss.

A full moon----Joy. A full moon with a sky of stars in Tucson----Bliss.

Attending a movie, play or concert----Joy. Attending a good movie, play or concert----Bliss.

A round of golf----Joy. A hole in one----Bliss.

Told that I am loved----Joy. Told that I am loved by my wife or grandchildren----Bliss.

Loving those close to me----Joy. Loving my wife----Bliss.

Taking off on an airplane----Joy. Landing----Bliss.

These are some of the pleasures in my life that evoke joy and bliss. I hope that I stimulated some of yours. A final example of exquisite joy and bliss in my life is

Attending the SaddleBrooke Writer's Group----Joy. Hearing readings that evoke laughter or crying or goose bumps----Bliss.

Lisa M. Cole

Wishbone Bush

(Mirabilis bigelovvi)*

Wishbone bush is a sprawling perennial of rocky slopes. It blooms in Spring and sometimes again in Fall.

It wasn't supposed to happen like this:
    I feel water on the edge of things. And then—water everywhere—
nothing new can bloom.

Born in pairs, the triangular or heart-shaped leaves are rather large and soft for the desert, so the plants generally do best when growing in the shade of shrubs or overhanging boulders.

The animal in you wants the animal in me—so
        sing the song of the common sparrow.
                Pull the coiled rope. Pull the night. Pull the road—Protect me.
                Do not wilt me.

Even then, wishbone bush is apt to wilt on hot days and to lose its leaves during long dry spells.

My heart closes—a fist,
    a dried petal. For once, it is smaller than water.

Staked glands, barely visible to the naked eye, make the leaves and stems feel tacky or even clammy to the touch. The white or pale pink flowers open late in the afternoon.

        Know that my wing cannot hinder (y)our unfolding:

Flowers typically comprise a certain number of petals set inside a certain number of sepals. The petals, taken collectively are the corolla; similarly the sepals are calyx.

Look on this land with eyes like tiny planets.
Harness this ink—lady day;
      lady bird;
           lady of the desert.

We think of petals as being brightly colored, sepals as being green. Wishbone bush, along with several other members of the 4'O'Clock Family flouts this convention.

Now—make a wish.

Because the funnel shaped flowers of the wishbone bush are actually fused sepals, each flower is a calyx. Despite appearances to the contrary, wishbone bush has no petals, and therefore no corolla.

And still—
      the darkness will take what it takes. The darkness has no family. The darkness has no water. The darkness does not bloom.

---

* Italicized portions taken from *Flowers and Shrubs of the Mojave Desert* by Janice Emily Bowers.

Kari Infantino

Without you

Last night I was so alone
The room so vast like outer space
The bed floating by strange dark planets
As I faced the blackness of your absence.

I slowly stacked the pillows on your side
In a straight vertical row
Like mounds of soft dried sand
With no apparent bones.

Your picture is propped on the pillow
Smiling with your warm dark eyes.
Now you are sleeping beside me
Together again as we travel one last time

Passing though different moons
My arm wrapped around our soft dreams
Kissing your paper cheeks
Moving through the immensity
For this, our last night together.

M. C. Little

DROUGHTS

Emergency! Lost crops…
        a "tinder box" they say.
With drought so hard upon us,
        will monsoons come today?

Dust harvests dust once more,
        grass brown as kiwi skin;
Prayers, politics and withered trees,
        soon water wars begin.

Bowl of mid-west top soil,
        blown off the dust-drenched plains,
Folks tasted it in mid-flight,
        in frenzied search for rain.

Lost colonies of Jamestown
        and Roanoke tree rings read:
"A dearth severe once lodged here
        and fed five-thousand dead."

Sunrise meets "sin agua"
        day-long desert answer,
Rhythms once more chanting…
        Anasazi dancer.

M. C. Little

BOUGAINVILLEA

Propelled by green-leafed branches
    Bougainvillea riots –
  Scarlet, violet, magenta brilliance,
Altogether reaching, spreading, spilling over
    Still beige stucco walls.

Annie Maud

The Dress

Silver.

Not grey,

Metallic threads of silver.

Sparkling, iridescent, capturing light and whispering it about as I moved.

I was 14, and still believed in magic. And the dress was magic.

In it I was graceful, beautiful, regal, and poised.

I could flirt, something I could never do in my plaid skirts and starched white blouses with the Peter-Pan collars.

I could smile little half-formed smiles, and flutter them at my beaux through darkened lashes.

When I danced I was air, wisps of smoke, promises of dusk and hidden excitement.

And, after the dance, alone in my darkened room, as I stripped off the dress in one swift movement:

Sparks of silver flashed, electricity spangled the air, fire danced in my hair!

Ah, the beauty of that one moment.

Magic.

Annie Maud

The Box

Up in the attic of my mind
Tucked away beneath the eaves
is a single box.

Wrapped, taped, tied tightly with heavy, knotted rope.

Threaded with spidery webs of anquish
wrinkled with the memory of painful tears.

Don't look! Don't go there!
As long as it remains untouched I can survive
I can forget
Someday, perhaps, even love again.

Elaine Mickelson Stamm

Weathering the Weather

Do you weather the weather with a coat and a hat?
It all depends on where you're <u>at</u>!
If in Alaska, I think you will---
And add to that---scarves to the gill.

But, if you're in Bali, it's a different thing---
Two fig leaves and one bikini string
Will give you comfort, but as you'll learn,
That'll also give you one heck of a burn!

In the Great Northwest, you're in puddles of rain---
In need of galoshes, umbrellas---the pain
Of curling your hair three times a day
Until you've had it and scream and say,
"Husband, it's time to go to the South!"
His bags were packed 'fore that left my mouth.

Whether to go, or whether to stay
Never came up, so we're here today---
SaddleBrooke, that is, in case you wonder.
We love all of its weather---even the thunder!

Amy Ouzoonian

On Letting Sleeping Dogs Lie

It's not time to leave his splendiferous feathers
Dozing. My thighs attempt temptation and storming
Outside it's 7 am and still breath and cloud formations.
Arizona precipitates cold sweat. Not ready for steam
Of showers and the shivers of dreams weave
Me out of bed wondering if I've left your arms
To fold frozen too often or if overstaying this visit
Has buried beads of laughter somewhere
In the backyard for the chickens to peck
And play their scratching game.
They uncover the comforter
And I slip further, sleepwalking into
A working day.

Charles Portolano

Coyote

In the light of day
coming out
of the wash,
he crosses the road
with a slight limp,
right in front
of my car
forcing me
to a full stop,
staring me down
with such distrust
almost contempt
for he knows
of our desire
to destroy him,
but by adapting
he out-smarted us,
now flourishing
among us,
he turns his back
to me, crossing
the asphalt road,
his bushy tail
shoots straight up,
stiff as only
a true dissident
would dare to do,
and with a wave
of his bushy tail
he disappears
into the wash
on the other side
of the road:
I had to laugh.

David Willing

A Morning's Palette

A pink hibiscus dawn opened
petal by petal.

David Willing

A Threaded Needle

Your teasing,
your embracing laugh
and silky smile
I resisted,
but your tears
and trembling heart
found me.

David Willing

White, Weightless Light

angels
have
no bones
hands
or
eyes
nothing burdening
only
weightless love

Michael Gessner
Published in The Yale Journal for Humanities in Medicine

Washed Out

My father stands in boxers,
back to the sea. He holds
my hand. I am five. We are a pair
on this Florida beach. We've remained
for years this way in black and white.

At forty-seven he looks 'washed out',
a phrase I learned from him,
used by a generation without pigment
spray, or tanning booths, to explain
the pallor of the face in age,
its waxiness from lack of circulation,
its corollaries in cotton fabrics hung
too long in the sun,
or what hurricanes do to ports,
and the conch on the beach
bleached of color.

He was no longer 'in the pink',
as his childhood chums would say
of each other when flushed
with health and expectation,
but not washed up, either,
not like the bloated things
that bellied-up and were pushed
away by tides, the undesirable
forms on the sand we stepped around.

Still we are here,
squinting against the sun,
still casting shadows.
In a few years I learned another phrase,
'Life is cheap,' he'd say,
Odd, for one who held it so near.

Charles Portolano

Time in the Desert

Hot here on summer afternoons;
stunning in the mornings and
the nights, fine times for a swim.

When the monsoons hit, first
light rain, thunder and lightning;
quite cool before the deluge of rain…

Two adult quail sail by
with eight tiny creepers in tow
across the street where we live.

Get a little green in the fall,
after the rains, fear of fire,
as the tumbleweeds fill the air.

Gets cold early on winter mornings,
great time to take a brisk walk, then
sit on the porch, soaking in the sun…

Spring goes green again, fast,
when the rains come, the world
around comes alive with color.

I listen closely in the early evenings
for the call of the coyotes coming
form the shadows of the saguaros,

with each passing year, harder to hear…

Melanie McCuin

To the Novelist from Boston
(Who Said, *If You Want to Be a Writer, You Can't Live in Arizona*)

My father was a poet.
In his lifetime, he grew a thousand skins, and like a tarantula crawling
    along the roads, shining blue, naked, he died in summer.
It's true,
that Arizonans speak the language of the dead: sunsets over mesas, fish
    bones resting in mudless buckets, dried roses, dried tulips, and
    dried peonies.
Women wear burned skins to bed and wake as blades of grass wilted
    onto asphalt, saguaros eaten away by claw and beak, or men
    who chase storms.

My father loved lightning, and one monsoon season we took his truck so
    far from the city, the horizon mirrored the surface of the moon.
We have to think like the clouds, he said, *move with them, get ahead of*
    them, stand in front of them and wait for the crackle-webs of
    light to unravel.
He drove fast through places with no signs, with no neon stars, with no
    windows left glowing for loved ones missing.
For miles, there was only night.
The clouds were somewhere ahead of us, stacking themselves high, and I
    could feel the absence of coyotes and breathe.

Then a flash blasted the horizon.
My father gunned it down the 134, 'til we reached a field of scrub brush
    and rock.
He opened the door of his truck, threw one foot onto soil, and then
    another, until he was in the middle of it.

My father called down the monsoon.
A gangly god with arms outstretched, mouth wide,
    he called down the bolts,
        he called down the wind,
            he called down the dust.
And when the floods came, he drank.

William Killian

There's Got to be a Better Place…

When the wind whipped me out of Indiana
I vowed I would never return.
Acts of God were no less fierce in the desert –
Homes washed away in the Tucson flood of '83 –
But I could no longer stand the devastation.
Winters didn't help, nor did the overcast skies
Ever bring comfort, and the humidity,
Flies, mosquitoes, and bible-belt mentality
Led me to a home away from home.

I now relive my Hoosier days at the 10 o'clock news –
Tornadoes rip through small towns
And devour poor souls
Who barely eke out a living
In areas where General Motors went silent.

In the dead of winter
I shake my head in disbelief
That I once slid from road to ditch,
Then flung dangerously back to traffic
Where I barely made it home.
Then in early a.m.
I would have to dig down deep to find my car,
Swearing *there's got to be a better place*.

My time now has over 300 days a year
Of perfect blue skies.
The mosquitoes I see die from loneliness,
The flies never crowd my life
Like they did in Koontz Lake, Indiana.
My sweat now is from honest heat,
Not from a moisture that never stops.

I have found, however, that the bible-belt
Stretches itself across the land,
And the lunatic politics of midwestern power
Do not come close to the idiocy of Arizona civics.

In my older age,
I don't know if the chaotic hot air out of Phoenix
Will send me packing to yet another home,
But I doubt it.

Today, Saturday, March 03, 2012

Was a perfectly magnificent day.
The sunset tonight
Will appear in an issue of *Arizona Highways*,
And the poor souls in Indiana
Will swear it's a painting, not a photograph
As they slam the phone
When we talk too much of our desert life.

Hawkeye Watkins

Coyote Whisper

Whisper was a Doberman mix.
Experts told me she was Rottweiler,
Or Labrador, for this reason or that.
They were experts. She was a good dog.

As a pup, from a rescue shelter,
I had her about six weeks before I named her.
Or she named herself. She never barked.
It finally hit me. "Whisper," I picked her up and kissed her.

She was really fast, faster than her breed should be.
At the dog park she would out run almost all other dogs.
Except the Greyhounds. Once they got going, it was no comparison.
Still, she was extremely fast.

And she loved chasing that tennis ball.
I had one of those plastic tennis ball throwers.
I would heave the ball as far as I could.
She would tear it up chasing that ball, 'til I got tired.

I worked graveyard shift. At 2 a.m.
I would take her to the park, a huge baseball-soccer field.
The time wasn't odd. Not for me. Not for her.
Not to worry, I picked up after her.

This one night, I was throwing the ball with her.
The park lights were on, making a globe of light
That receded into darkness. I would watch as the ball
Arced away, far out of my vision.

She would spin and bolt off,
Her black and tan coat quickly disappearing
As she left the circle of light
Chasing down that escaping yellow orb.

This one time, she took a long time to come back.
I called to her, but she didn't come.
Figuring the ball had gone down a drain, or got stuck somewhere,
I started walking forward, to help her out.

Suddenly, she came trotting back, ball in mouth.
I smiled, "Good girl." Then I frowned.
Something moved at the edge of the light.
My nerves got on edge. Something was out there.

I peered into the dark.
Hard.
Petting Whisper,
I saw it.

Clearly not a dog.
It was a coyote,
Moving just at the edge of the light.
All my senses lit up.

My mind said, "Fear the pack!"
I scanned around us. Nothing was there.
But something inside me sent a different signal.
Something inside was saying it was okay.

I listened to that second voice, for often it has been truer.
I walked forward to the edge of the light.
Every step I took forward,
The coyote retreated, but no farther.

I turned around and walked back into the light,
Whisper still heeling at my side.
When I got to the center, I turned around.
The coyote was RIGHT THERE!

Not a foot from me, not two inches from Whisper.
I hadn't heard a sound.
It scampered back a few feet, then just looked at me.
Or smiled.

One last time, my mind said,
"It's trying to lure you into the open,
Or into the dark, where the pack is waiting."
But my heart just knew better. I can't explain it better.

I tossed the ball a short distance,
Landing in the light.
Whisper streaked for it, got it, and came back.
The coyote shadowed her, silent and infinitely quicker.

This continued. I started tossing the ball farther and farther,
Finally chucking it as far as I could, off into the darkness.
Coyote never left her side, never interfered with her.
Whisper didn't mind.

We played like this for hours.
Literally hours.
Me amused, bewildered,
Whisper happy, coyote shadowing her.

The sun started to rise and I had to go.
When I called Whisper to me the final time
And started for the car,
Coyote knew. He trotted off towards the woods near the park.

I stopped at my car. He stopped at wood's edge.
We looked at one another, smiled at the *enemy*,
Briefly friend's in time,
He went his way, I went mine.

Hawkeye Watkins

Have You Ever Heard the Sound of Nothing?

I worked a summer at Katmai National Park.
Called that because when the volcano blew half the mountain away
Everyone thought it was Mt. Katmai.
It wasn't, but it's named that still.

Internationally famous for fishing and bears,
It can only be reached by boat or plane, mostly plane.
Truth is, many of the famous photos and videos
You have seen of Grizzlies were taken there.

Most of the visitors are wealthy Europeans,
Or eccentric Americans. Dabbled into the mix are the photo-fanatics,
And those seeking a little adventure, and those wanting to experience
The wild unlike the wild anywhere else.

One of my many tasks was to get the main lodge opened up in the
Morning. Every night, a sow would bring her three cubs into camp to
Protect them 'cuz the boars wouldn't come in. Every morning I had to
Find her and her cubs, just to make sure we were still on friendly terms.

A river runs beside the main cabin area.
The bears would come in to fish the river.
Daily, I would encounter these bears,
Often not more than a few feet away.

I don't say these things to brag, although a little bragging may be due.
I say them to express to you that while I am not the person
Most familiar with Grizzlies,
I certainly am more familiar than most.

So when I tell you that a bear is huge,
You know I'm not just blowin' smoke.
You'll know I speak from experience.
That'll make sense later.

Having done my share of working,
I earned a few days off.
I decided to hike up to the steam vents
And take a sauna.

When the volcano exploded, and the lava cooled,
It left a 15 mile long, 9 mile wide lava flow.
Still hot underneath, in places, the steam vents up to the surface.
In places, there are tarps, and those who know can take a sauna.

So I slipped on my backpack, my knife,
Picked up my walking staff and headed out on the trail.
Leaving the camp, leaving the woods, I finally got to the flow,
And started the multi-mile trek.

Where the animals, and occasional human, walk on the flow
It grinds the lava down, making a worn trail.
I followed this for hours. For miles.
Hot, sweaty, I decided to take a break.

I scanned around. In the distance, the mountain ranges ranged in all
Directions. Before me were miles of brown, empty lava. Behind me,
More of the same.
Beside me, more of the same, in both directions.

Then I had a thought.
I have never heard the sound of nothing.
There was no wildlife, no wind, no planes, no cars, no radios,
No insects, no nothing. Except for me, absolute silence.

"How cool it would be to hear absolutely nothing,"
I thought to myself.
So I propped my walking staff into the ground, giving me something to
Lean on. I tried to stop moving, but I just couldn't.

May seem odd, but when there is absolutely no other sound, you may be
Surprised at how much noise you make. My clothing was rubbing, my
Boots made just the slightest grinding sound as they rested on the lava.
It was frustrating that I couldn't make no noise.

Trying to be "silenter", I propped up my staff, leaned into it,
Resting my backpack and weight into it and my legs.
This enabled me to remain absolutely still long enough to hear…
To hear the sound of nothing!

It was amazing.
It was so simple, and so amazing.
I was so happy, joyful.
Then something happened.

Just like you read about, the hairs on the back of my neck stood up.
I had an overwhelming sense of dread, that I was being watched.
I looked up.
Walking down the trail, the worn trail, directly at me, was a Grizzly.

A huge Grizzly.
Remember earlier, when I said something would make sense later?
That later is now.
It was a HUGE Grizzly. By far, the largest I have ever seen.

If you've never been in the wild with an animal that can end you,
That sensation is hard to describe. It isn't like being at a zoo and
Wondering. It isn't like coming across a deer, or some other animal.
It is… humbling.

The next few thoughts and actions happened in slow motion, and in a
Split second.
> The Grizzly is face down, walking directly at me.
> He is about 60 feet away.
> He is huge.
> Behind me is nine miles of open lava, nowhere to go.
> My god, he is huge.
> To my left is four miles of open lava, nowhere to go.
> Briefly, I thought of my knife, immediately scoffing.
> To my right is four miles of open lava, nowhere to go.
> That's the biggest bear I've ever seen.
> The slight wind is blowing toward me, not good. NOT GOOD.
> Don't surprise him. Let him know you are here.

"Hey, Bear!"
"Hey, Bear!" I drop my backpack.
"Hey, Bear!" arms waving.
    Great, he can't hear me.
    One last look around, nowhere to go.
    I do not want to startle this bear.
    From somewhere I think of my harmonica.

No, I can't play the harp.
Not like someone who can play.
I carried it around for when I was solo hiking
And no one would be able to hear me.

I pulled it out of my front pocket.
Thinking low notes would travel better,
I blew on it hard.
Plod, plod, the bear kept walking toward me, now 30 feet away.

Near panic, I blew the high note.
Now, I gotta tell ya,
And I'm not making this up,
But that bear skidded.

It was like a cartoon.
He locked up all four legs
And just skidded across the lava
For a few feet.

He was about 20 feet from me now.
I knew there was nowhere to run.
Hell, he could outrun a deer, let alone a lowly human.
I knew if he wanted me I was his.

He rose up onto his hinds legs.
He was huge.
I say again, not because of proximity,
He was huge.

He looked me up and down.
I just stood there and said to myself and him,
"I got nowhere to go. If you want to eat me, or kill me,
Or just smack me around, I'm yours."

I remember an intense feeling of majesty.
Not mine.
His.
It is the strongest impression I was left with.

Finally, he slowly lowered himself down to all fours.
He then turned to a side, and walked around me.
Exactly. If you took a length of rope, pinned it where I was,
And drew a circle, that was the exact path he took.

As he got back on the path, now behind me,
I think I realized that I hadn't been breathing.
Or at least not much. I sighed and said,
"Damn, that bear was huge."

Edward Dobson

They Gathered Again

They gathered again, as they had once a year for the last fifty years.
Not in thousands like at first, or even hundreds like twenty years ago.
But eleven now alive, all over eighty-five.
Some in wheeled conveyances, some struggling with walkers with
    aluminum joints.
The factory, abandoned these sixty years.
Decaying, rusting, collapsing, the roof showing the night sky.
All hushed, expectant, tense.
The chain to be pulled at midnight.
The last bulb hung there, gently in the star light,
Its tungsten filament miraculously unmelted, when all the billions of
    others had died out more than fifty years ago.
Had blazed their last, burnt out, gone.
Now a lost technology only remembered by the eleven.
Incandescence was a travesty in those days, a crime to own, to burn that
    much electricity.
Prison for possession.
But this one hundred watt bulb discovered hidden.
Forgotten, in an ancient, steel drawer in the abandoned factory.
Found and twisted into a cobweb covered socket and lit.
Fifty years ago.
Lit again secretly once every year on the date of the death of
    Thomas Alva Edison, at midnight.
And now, a hand reaching to grasp the tiny rusted chain.
The signal given, the shaking fingers seeking the chain, hesitantly
    pulling.
The bulb flashed, for a second, then popped in a super nova of light and
    died.
Those ancient ones, left standing in the star light, many in tears,
    understanding the symbolism of the bulb.
Yet stunned,
They themselves to burn out forgotten in the fullness of time.

Elizabeth H. Tilley

The History Books

We will be known in history books.
Our flashing smiles and daring dreams
held together with unforgettable good looks.
If only for a little while, we will.
We have danced and are damned
just like all the rest.
Yes, we will be known, written about,
and discussed in a scholarly manner.
Bored eyes will take in our lives
and hope to pass the test on Friday.
But our walks on silver
moonlit pathways shall be unknown.
Fragile conversations with close friends – lost.
Dancing and laughing, holding hands,
and essence emerging as we move to live music,
shall be subject to sober interpretation by the scribes.
Benjamin Franklin once longed for a girl
and wanted to ask her to dance,
but no one ever knew.
He hid his desire in clever quotes
caught by critics and used for
educational purposes.
If only the history books could capture
the driving desire that moved him forward,
broke his heart, and made him the man
on paper we see today.
These moments, precious, distinct,
and meaning more than
the sum of their parts, gone.
And only the history books will show
the cardboard cut-outs of lives,
penny people chasing places.
And the soft hum of crickets,
bringing me to tears,
as I stand in awe of the vastness,
shall never be mentioned.

Betty Canavan

The Holiday Horseman

Once upon a time in Arizona, where the tall Saguaro cacti grow;
Weather started getting much cooler, way down to 40 or so.
Horses were looking kinda fuzzy, hanging far away in a herd;
In the quiet of the evening, all nature's sounds were blurred.

I made my way into the bunkhouse, opened up my faithful old trunk;
Hunted and found my favorite long-johns, man, them things sure stunk!
Took them and hung them on the porch rail, thought they would probably air out;
Stud that was sleeping in the round pen, curled up his lip and ran about.

Got up real early next mornin', put on a big pot of Joe;
When that old coffee got to smellin', dropped in a couple eggs or so.
Walking around the bunk half-naked, knees took to rattlin' pretty hard;
And, if you never did see them, they were the color of lard.

Went out and grabbed me up my long-johns, don't want you all to be misled;
But, in the early morning sunshine, they glowed a really bright red.
Now, these things weren't silk or latex, they didn't have no controls;
When I pulled them up on my body, they had a hundred old holes.

So, I forgot and put my clothes on, to go out and split me some wood;
Stacked a load over by the fireplace, another by the kitchen stove hood.
Scattered a bale for the horses, chipped all the ice on the trough;
Went to the barn and milked the old cow, checked on her calf with the cough.

Day was a breakin' mighty pretty, it was preparin' to snow;
This was the day before Christmas, so into town I would go.
Checked out my cash in my pockets, rounded up the keys to my truck;
I'd get to town in an hour and back before the snow with some luck.

I tipped my hat to the ladies, as I went in the Mercantile;
Headed straight over to the long-johns, picked up a pair with a smile.
Took them over to the checkout, "Could I pay and please wear 'em home?"
"Sure" with a smile from the salesgirl, "Here is your free pocket comb."

I felt so good I can't describe it, hadn't felt this good in many years;
If I weren't such a tough old wrangler, this would have brought me to tears.
I stopped to talk with my buddies, they shared a pinch of their chew;
We talked the same old gossip, added a couple things new.

I made it home before the snowfall, had time to finish my chores;
Made me a lovely warm supper, had coffee on the porch outdoors.
I was a feelin' so cozy, startin' to fall off to sleep;
Thought I had better get inside now, 'afore I was countin' them sheep.

Hell, how could my day be so ruined, how did I slam the damn door?
My keys were still in my pockets, layin' on the living room floor.
There I was, standing in the twilight, without a jacket on me;
Wearin' my brand new long-johns, now I really had to pee.

Raised up the hood on my old truck, it only let out a groan;
Now, I was getting a little cranky, standing there all alone.
Moon rising over the hillside, evening was startin' to commence;
I peered out over my shoulder, my horses were lined up at the fence.

If anybody could see them, they'd say those horses could speak;
Looked like the filly winked at me, looked like the mare gave her critique.
Went to the barn and grabbed my saddle, tied up my favorite stud;
Turned 'round and knocked my good pad down, now it was sittin' in the mud.

Tore off a piece of my old long-johns, lay out a piece on his back;
Tied off the leg of another, making it into a sack.
Just then an idea popped in my head, i thought I was gettin' smart;
I started rippin' up them long-johns, taking them all apart.

One piece I made into a small hat, one piece became a saddle pad;
One piece fit over my studs head, he didn't look too bad.
Put my jeans on as a jacket, rode to the neighbors through the snow;
As my place grew smaller in the distance, it really started in to blow.

I saw the light there over yonder, my blood was getting very thin;
I saw a tree in their window, I couldn't wait to get in.
There were the youngun's in the window, then they suddenly disappeared;
Snow had stuck all over my body, making a big white beard.

Everyone ran out to greet me, laughing and giving me applause;
For I was the Holiday Horseman, looking like old Santa Claus.
Now, here's the twist in my story, remember the Mercantile store?
That salesgirl really did like me, she packed a comb and much more.

Suckers were packed for everybody, there were some candy canes, too;
Pocket combs and ginger bread cookies, enough gum for everyone to chew.
Well, if I ever were to marry, this is how I'd like it to be;
Having an angel like my neighbor did, on everything they agree.

That lady took my clothes and dried them, put hot water in the bath tub;
Wrapped me up in a big blanket, fed me a plate of hot grub.
Christmas mornin' after breakfast, he loaded my horse and drove us home;
And, for a special Christmas present, gave me my own cell phone.

Ann Kuperberg

Purple Passion

I am small and delicate.
There is a regal demeanor about me, yet some people see passion
      in my coloring.
I can be your best friend. Whisper sweet thoughts to me.
Tell me your secrets. I will share your joys and sorrows.
Sing to me, scream your frustrations, I will listen.
I will be your constant companion. Come and go as you please.
I will always be home waiting patiently for you.
On dreary days, I will lighten your spirits.
On sunny days, I will stir spurts of energy in your veins.
I am your soul-mate. All I ask in return is food and shelter.
Give me the sun's warmth without its scorching intensity.
Give me proper nourishment without extremes.
I can be housed in artificial light or in natural rays streaming
      through a windowpane.
I'm not very demanding. I will flourish.
As in all life, moderation is the key to survival.
If you feed me too little, I will wilt.
If you feed me too much, I will drown.
Every so often I will crave extra vitamins to help me shine.
I will give you unconditional love and beauty.
My delicate loveliness will blossom in my soft purple petals,
      sunny yellow buds and velvety green heart-shaped leaves.
Once you have loved me, you will love no other in the same way.
My purple passion will always remain.
I am an African violet.

Carol Hogan

Ocean

Ocean, her name was Ocean
Dark as coffee
Skin like burnished wood
Her laugh clear as crystal bells
Making new my second-hand heart
Ocean, brown velvet pillows
Around my heart she throws
Tender sighs from knowing eyes
Surprising, engaging, stealing-my-heart --
Startling blue
They hold me still
Ocean, her name was Ocean

Stuart Watkins

One God, One World, One People

One God,
One World,
One People.
And, whether your pain
Comes from a Tsunami,
Earthquake, Fire, Storm,
Or Soldiers killing Citizens;
One People,
One World,
One God.

Translated by Maria Rodriguez-Pope

Un Dios, Un Mundo, Un Pueblo

Un Dios,
Un Mundo,
Un Pueblo,
Y, aunque tu dolor
Venga de un sunami,
Terremoto, fuego, tormenta,
O solidados matando a la gente;
Un Pueblo,
Un Mundo,
Un Dios.

Translated by Ingrid Dalton

Ein Gott, Eine Welt, Ein Volk

Ein Gott,
Eine Welt,
Ein Volk,
Und, ob Dein Schmerz
Verursacht wurde von einer Tsunami,
Erdbeben, Feuer, Sturm,
Oder von Soldaten, die Bürger töten;
Ein Volk,
Eine Welt,
Ein Gott.

Greek Translation of
"One God, One World, One People"

The translation was done by Rip Economou
The typing was done by Maria Berry
And Bill Anastopoulus put it all together.

Ένας θεός

Ένας κόσμος

Ένας λαός

Και είτε ο πόνος σού

Είναι από τρικυμία

Σεισμού, πυρκαγία, η θύελλα,

Ένας λαός

Ένας κόσμος

Ένας θεός

Один Бог, Один Мир, Один Народ

(Стьюарт Уоткинс)

Один Бог,

Один Мир,

Один Народ,

Откуда бы твоя боль не пришла -

Цунами, землетрясения, пожары, ураганы

Или из-за солдат, убивающих мирных граждан;

Один Народ,

Один Мир,

Один Бог.

(This poem was translated into Russian

by Daria Sergeeva,

A member of I Liq Chuan.)

Arizona Land, Ranch, and Farm Agents

If you ever bought or sold a ranch, farm, or land in Arizona, you probably dealt with some of these real estate agents. This page is a tribute to those agents, most of whom belong to the oldest real estate exchange group in the United States. This Tucson group is called TREE (Tucson Real Estate Exchangors). If you want to look up the current membership, please go to:
www.tucsonrealestateexchangers.com

Tucson:	Steve Latham	**Mesa:**
Craig Abbott	Dorothy Love	Dave Hillger
Bill Anastopoulus	Mario Raso	**Mt. Lemon:**
George Beasley	Mark Ross	Bob Zimmerman
Ingrid Dalton	Everett Rothrock	**Pierce:**
Lee Davis	Cassius Sargent	Bill Dawson
Alan Friedman	Tom Starrs	Vince Hutson
George Grizwold	Stuart Watkins	**Sierra Vista:**
Betty Hannon	John Weaver	Bob Watkins
Joe Heater	**Bisbee:**	**Tempe:**
Ed Henney	Charles Sotelo	Larry E. Sarkis
Jim Hogan	**Casas Grande:**	Steve Thomas
Gloria Jackson	Joe Sul	**Wickenburg:**
Mike Kauffman	**Gilbert:**	Bob Harvey
Art Kelley	Roxane Mojher	

This list is meant to represent those active land, farm, and ranch agents still residing in Arizona, and I did not mean to slight anyone. If I left someone out by accident, I apologize.

Arizona's Native American Tribes

Arizona is home to 21 federally recognized tribes. Arizona has about 250,000 Native Americans. Reservations and tribal communities comprise about a fourth of Arizona's lands. They are such a part of the history of this whole area they deserve to be recognized in this book.

- Ah-Chin Indian Community
- Yavapai-Apache Nation
- Navajo Nation
- Cocopah Indian Reservation
- Colorado River Indian Tribes
- White Mountain Apache Tribe
- Fort McDowell Yavapai Nation
- Fort Mojave Indian Tribe
- Gila river Indian Community
- Havasupai Indian Reservation
- Hopi Tribe
- Hualapai Tribe
- Kaibab-Pauite Tribe
- Pascua Yaqui Tribe
- Salt River Pima-Maricopa Community
- San Carlos Apache Reservation
- Tohono O'odham Nation
- Tonto Apache Tribe
- Yavapai-Prescott Indian Tribe
- Fort Yuma-Quechan Tribe
- San Juan southern Paiute Tribe

Works Cited

Editor's Note: Information is as provided by the Poet; I'm okay with that. Some Poets did not provide the requested information by press time.

Buntin, Simmons. "Arc." *Freshwater* (Asnuntuck Community College). Enfield, Connecticut : 2010. Journal.

Crume, Mary. "Caught in a Mirage." *Mood Swings.* Scottsdale, Arizona : Self-published, 2009. Print.

Davison, Don. "A Mountain Man." *Iris and Other Things: A Collection.* Tempe, Arizona : Zirahuen Publishing, 2005/2010. Print.

Gessner, Michael. "Washed Out." *The Yale Journal for Humanities in Medicine.* December 12, 2011, <http://yjhm.yale.edu/poetry/mgessner20111212.htm>. Web.

Gigstad, Peggy. "Monsoon Minute." *Harmony, a humanities magazine.* Tucson, Arizona : Arizona Health Science Center, 2009. Print.

Gigstad, Peggy. "Speedway and Campbell." *Harmony, a humanities magazine.* Tucson, Arizona : Arizona Health Science Center, 2008. Print.

Hoagland, Archie. "Desert Sunrise." *The Collection.* Indian Trail, North Carolina : D-N Publishing, 2010. Print.

Hoagland, Archie. "Farmer." *The Collection.* Indian Trail, North Carolina : D-N Publishing, 2010. Print.

Joiner, Leila. "Leaving." *OASIS Journal.* Tucson, Arizona : Imago Press, 2002. Print.

Joiner, Leila. "Screwdriver." *OASIS Journal*. Tucson, Arizona : Imago Press, 2002. Print.

Killian, William. "Mothers Die at the Wrong Time." *All the Faces I Have Been: An Actor's Notebook.* Tucson, Arizona : Imago Press, 2010. Print.

Kuperberg, Ann. "Dear Wizard." *Yellow Bricks and Ruby Slippers.* McKinleyville, California : Daniel & Daniel Publishers, Inc. Print.

Kuperberg, Ann. "Purple Passion." *African Violet Magazine.* May-June, 1998. Print.

Needle, Burgess. "Grandfather Antonio." *Every Crow in the Blue Sky*. Ft. Worth, Texas : Diminuendo Press, 2009. Print.

Needle, Burgess. "Tucson Night." *Every Crow in the Blue Sky.* Ft. Worth, Texas : Diminuendo Press, 2009. Print.

Biographies

From Stuart: Here is some information about some of the poets in this book. Some poets never submitted information. I apologize if you were omitted by mistake.

Note from the Editor: In the 1st Edition, the bios, although added, were not edited by the Editor. In this, the Revised Edition, while now edited, the bios are almost entirely statements provided by the poets and are just that, statements by the poets. They have not been verified, nor are they going to be. Some of the spelling and grammar, as in the poems, is the poet's choice. I'm okay with that. This is a book of poems, not a doctoral thesis, medical report, or an exposé on corporate crime. Like some Cowboy Poets may tell you about life, take it with a grain of salt, relax a little. You may find you enjoy it a little more.

Bob Adams is a long term member of the SaddleBrooke Writer's club.

Mark Bahti, a long-time Tucsonan, runs an Indian arts shop in Tucson and in Sante Fe. He is best known for his books and articles on Southwest Indian art, history, and culture. He is a Fellow of the Society for Applied Anthropology.

Dick Bakken is the first person allowed a creative M.A. thesis in English at Washington State University. He was the Director, Summer Writers Camp. Bisbee, AZ 1997. He has taught poetry in many states, has edited many books, and has won many awards.

Sally Bates has been so helpful in getting fellow poets to submit their poems. She is one of the persons behind all the Cowboy Poets in Arizona. "I was raised on a ranch near Prescott, and grew up with cowboys and their kind. My Dad and several of our friends recited poetry, sang cowboy songs, and passed on to me this "sacred trust" of keeping the tradition alive. That was my goal in helping establish and support cowboy poetry gatherings wherever my help and performance was requested. When they began to turn into another entertainment venue, and ceased being mostly about the culture and heritage of the American cowboy, I began returning to my roots. It is for this reason I no longer attend more than a handful of events each year, but I continue to write about the roots of my raising and share that with those who care about such things."

Gerald (Jerry) Bigelow is a retired Information Technology executive and worked in the Aero Space Industry. He started a poetry club in Tucson that meets monthly called S.O.A.P.

Dr. Leonard Bischel wrote *Poetry, Beauty, and God* for the Fifteenth World Congress of Poets July 21-23, 1997 Buckinghamshire College, High Wycombe, Buckingham, England.

Bonita Blankenship has had several articles published in SaddleBrooke's newspaper, *SaddleBag Notes*. She has two self-printed books. One is about the 11 years as a missionary in Peru and Brazil with Wycliffe Bible Translators, and another, *Roots and Offshoots*, with ancestral stories, featuring a short story of her great grandparents' romance after the Civil War.

JoAnn Breul says, "I used to write when I was young and carefree, but then the realities of life shelved those dreams. I started writing poetry many years later during a very dark period of my life. I found it directed my pain and gave me an outlet for my dark thoughts. Then one day I started to dream again. My poems reflected those moments of hope. Eventually a shift occurred and I was finally free of the dark. I was afraid that it was only my pain that was the muse and was nervous that my writing therapy days were over. But low and behold I discovered that love, happiness, and hope made for great musings as well. So I write. I can't not write. I have to express my deepest thoughts because now I am in touch with my true inner self, and she has lots of things to say! I am a teacher by trade. I substitute teach in the Alhambra School District. I feel it is my calling to be a positive influence in the lives of children. I have three teenage boys of my own, all living at home!

Rhonda Brown is an Arizona transplant who finds abundant poetic inspiration in Arizona's natural phenomena.

Les Buffham: Western Music Association Songwriter of the Year, Academy of Western Artists Song of the Year, Western Music Association Poet of the Year, 2007,2008, Western Music Association Song Collaboration of the Year, 2009, Academy of Western Artist-storyteller-humorist. He has two CD's: *Below the Kenney Rim* and *Writes and Co-Writes*.

Simmons B. Buntin is the founding editor of *Terrain.org: A Journal of the Built & Natural Environments*. His first book of poetry, *Riverfall*, was published in 2005 by Ireland's Salmon Poetry. His second collection, *Bloom*, was published by Salmon Poetry in 2010. His poetry has appeared in *Mid-American Review*, *Isotope*, *Orion*, *Hawk & Handsaw*, *Southwestern American Literature*, *High Desert Journal*, *ISLE*, *Freshwater*, *Kyoto Journal*, *Salamander*, *Versal*, and *North American Review*.

Patricia Bush wrote *These Hands* and the photograph was taken by her granddaughter, Emily Hagopian, a professional photographer. She spent 40 years in radio, TV, and advertising.

Karen B. Call wrote *People Watching at Discount Tire* while watching people there.

Shawn Cameron is a native Arizonan and professional artist whose oil paintings and poetry tell the story of contemporary ranch life. Her artwork has graced three posters for the Arizona Cowboy Poets Gathering in Prescott, AZ, where she has participated as a reciting poet. Her poetry is published in *Thanks for the Poems: A commemorative collection for the 20th Arizona Cowboy Poets Gathering*, published by Sharlot Hall Museum of Prescott, AZ. As a professional artist, she has participated in shows such as the Prix de West at Western Heritage and Cowboy Hall of Fame, OK City, OK; Cowgirl Up! at the Desert Caballeros Museum, Wickenburg, AZ; and the C. M. Russell Auction in Great Falls, MT. She is represented by Trailside Galleries in both Scottsdale, AZ, and Jackson, WY, and Tierney Fine Art in Bozeman, MT.

Betty Canavan is an amateur poet who writes personalized birthday greetings to her friends. She grew up in Dearborn, MI, where she worked in the library, then Ford Motor Company. She studied biology and interior design. She traveled 100,000 miles most of her life as president of a NASCAR racing team. She has been to the White House for dinner. Also, she was VP of an aftermarket auto parts firm. Later, she lived on a CA horse ranch, caring for 50 horses. She has been a member of General Federation of Woman's Clubs for 12 years, of which 4 years were spent on the board. She was on the vestry of two churches as well. Hoping she can assist caregivers, she is currently writing about the ten years she took care of her mother who suffered from Alzheimer's. She was able to get through it with a sense of humor. She also works at Bridle and Bit newspaper in Cave Creek, AZ, where she currently lives. She has three married daughters, two living in Cave Creek and one in Thompson, ND.

Jefferson Carter's works have appeared in *Carolina Quarterly*, *Sonora Review*, *Spork*, *Barrow Street*, and *New Poets of the American West*. Chax Press (Tucson) published *Sentimental Blue* (2007) and *My Kind of Animal* (2010). He volunteers for Sky Island Alliance.

Lola Chiantaretto lives on a small outfit (28,000 acres) with her husband, Harry. They spend most of their time keeping up with their cattle or one of their many family members. Having spent many years in other professions, Lola finally got a chance to realize her dream of cowboying in 1999. Since that time she has worked on 20 or more ranches in AZ and handled cattle of every temperament. She and Harry continue to ranch 25 miles south west of Bagdad, AZ, where she writes cowboy poetry in her spare time.

David Chorlton was born in Austria, grew up in England, and spent several years in Vienna before moving to Phoenix in 1978. His poetry collections include *Waiting for the Quetzal* and *The Porous Desert*. His newest book is a work of fiction with its origins in 1960s Vienna: *The Taste of Fog*, from Rain Mountain Press.

Lisa M. Cole is a full time writer who holds a MFA in poetry from the University of Arizona's Creative Writing program. She is the author of two chapbooks: *Tinder//Heart* and *The Bodyscape*, both of which are forthcoming from Dancing Girl Press.

James Cox is a member of the SaddleBrooke Writer's Club. He is a retired aerospace physicist. He is a Distinguished Member of the International Society of Poets and recognized as a Poet Laureate in that Society. His poems have appeared in fourteen chapbooks, newspapers, magazines and many anthologies. His published books *The Essence of Jim*, *As the Mood Prescribes*, and *Rubai* were all published by Authorhouse.

Mary S. Crume published *Caught in a Mirage* in a chapbook titled *Mood Swings* in 2009.

Ingrid Dalton was born in Germany and published *How to Get Rid of Your Clutter with an Easy 5-Step System*. She is the owner/broker of ACE Realty in Tucson.

Don Davison was born in northern Wisconsin, the son of a Forest Ranger and Tree Farmer. His mother was a newspaper secretary. He has had careers in counseling, consulting, and as a university professor. His wife, Patricia, takes most of the pictures for his books. He has published 6 volumes of poetry (with two more in the pipeline) and 3 volumes of essays (with another on its way). All are available on Amazon.

Rod Drought has been published in various small press poetry anthologies for over 30 years. He is also a drummer/songwriter/singer in the band WYSIWYG.

Edward Dobson is a member of the SaddleBrooke Writer's Club.

Jay Dusard gave me several photos that I hope get included in this book. The Hughes Men at the Diamond 2 Ranch in 1984 is a classic. Arizona highways published his photo *Buster Scarbrough and Bob Pulley, A Bar V Ranch, Skull Valley, AZ 1981* in the December 2011 edition. He is a writer and photographer out of Douglas, AZ.

Richard Dyer attended Chouinard Art Institute in Los Angeles, CA. After two years in the Army, he began a 35-year career as a rancher in Southern California, while pursuing his interest in art on the side. He studied under John Collier, an artist of note, who specialized in landscapes, seascapes, and portraits in oil. Bill Powell extended Mr. Dyer's talent in the same medium in a more structured discipline. Long-time friend and mentor Gene Franks refined his sketching technique and multiple subject composition in acrylics and dry brush watercolor. Mr. Dyer currently exhibits his work in Tucson and Scottsdale, AZ, and Palm Desert, CA. While some of his work reflects his years on the ranch, his work covers a wide variety of subjects including landscapes, seascapes, portraits, and wildlife.

J. P. Ellsworth wrote *The Story of C. C. Hall* which was published in *The Straight Scoop*. This poem came about from his reading a book by Edmond Wells, *Argonaut Tales of Edmond Wells*. Phil read the article and put it into rhyme.

Barbara Evans worked for JetBlue. She wrote *What Babies Need* for a baby shower. She wrote a poem for one of the airline's birthday celebrations that won her some luggage and then named a plane "A Friend Like Blue" that won her an all-expenses-paid trip to Toulouse, France.

Jack Evans is a three time former President of the Arizona State Poetry Society. Over the years he has directed The Divergent Arts Series, Poetry in the Park, the Downtown Series, Dismantling the Silence and The Anthology Series in Mesa. Jack is co-director of the Caffeine Corridor Series with Shawnte Orion.

Erdeen Evertsen was born in 1924. She had four boys, four girls, six foster children, and sponsored 54 Hollanders after World War II. She is active in the LDS Church and enjoys life.

Rolf Flake has a great CD recording of his poems and songs, *Western Verse or Worse*. Rolf did not tell me much about himself, but other poets have. He is quite the Cowboy Poet.

Sandra Fortense is a former car dealer, rancher, and photographer. Photographing the peace and beauty of this beautiful world has inspired her to write the poem *A Gentle Breeze*, as well as many others.

Ona Lesa Foster has been writing since she was 16. She graduated Summa Cum Laude. She joined the Green Valley Poetry Society and the Valley Players. She has won many awards. She is now involved with the Tucson Poetry Festival and has studied with the Poet Laureate of New Mexico.

Robert A. Frost – Scottsdale's Honorary Poet Laureate two years running - is a cowboy poet. His writing is of the traditional story telling style of the old west. True to the tradition, some are humorous, others more serious and philosophic. He began writing poetry more than 50 years ago and continued through his career. Once retired, he published his poetry collection and later found a knack for writing Cowboy Poetry. He is often called upon to create original poems for special occasions and dedications. He is available to provide entertainment for your group, organization or gathering. He has won many awards, such as First Place in the Tombstone Cowboy Poetry Contest (2009), and has published two books, *A Sweet Place to Play* (2002) and *Cowboy Poems About the Old West and New* (2009).

Peggy Gigstad is a nurse educator, a retired colonel, and a poetry lover.

Michael Gessner's poems have been included in the *American Literary Review, The Journal of The American Medical Association,(JAMA), Oxford Magazine, Pacific Review, Poem, Sycamore Review, Wallace Stevens Journal* and others. His most recent collection is *Beast Book*, (Blazevox, 2010), and his latest review is "Imagining Poe" in the spring (2011) issue of *The Edgar Allan Poe Review*. Forthcoming poems (April, 2012) will appear in *Ann Arbor Review*, and *The French Literary Review*.

Michael Gregory's *Praxis* was previously published in the on-line journal *Fiera Lingue* and will be included in his collection, *Mr. America Drives his Car*, forthcoming in spring, 2012. One of the co-founders of the Bisbee Poetry Festival, he has published several poetry books, including *The Valley Floor, Hunger Weather 1959-1975*, and *re: Play*. Until retirement a few years ago, Michael was an internationally-recognized toxics activist working on right-to-know issues along the US-Mexico border and elsewhere. Since 1971 he has lived off-grid in the high desert grassland of southeastern Arizona.

Dan Gilmore wrote *Love Takes a Bow* which was published by Imago Press. Dan has received awards from Raymond Carver Fiction Contest, the Martindale fiction award, and SandScript.

Dean Guthery's poem *The Cowboy Way* was selected as C & I's Poem of the Week, 11-23-11. His wife adds art work to his writes. He told me stories about Bill Simon, Doc Pardee, Chuck Sheppard, Rusty Gibbons and tales about old Arizona. We had lunch at the I-Hop in Tucson.

Richard L. Hamilton is a SaddleBrooke resident and has published several historical Civil War books. A recent family tree search found he is related to Abraham Lincoln.

Larry Harmer is a long-time poet, performer, and hobbyist historian. The preservation of our western heritage is important to him. His poem, *There's a Poem in there Somewhere* is also the title to his CD.

Joseph Harris held both a MS and PhD in Neurochemistry. He spent a lifetime teaching and researching at the John Hopkins School of Medicine and the Arizona State University Department of Chemistry and Biochemistry. He was also a Fellow of the New York Academy of Science. He was a past President of the East Valley Poets and a former executive board member of the Arizona State

Poetry Society. United Poets International awarded him for his contributions to poetry. Joseph Harris passed away April 4, 2011. He was 91.

Alana Helapitage has written since she was a child. She has always found the written word to be like a second skin – to reflect, protect, and sustain who and what she is. Her influences include her relationships with loved ones, and Eastern and Western spirituality, philosophy, and psychology. Alana's work is comprised of mainly poetry, and also personal narratives and essays. This is Alana's second time being published, having been recently selected for *The Palo Verde Pages* (Volume 2, Issue 4) for her poem *Our Own Blood*.

Archie J. Hoagland, poet and author, was born at the height of the Great Depression of 1932. He grew up in the farmlands of Nebraska, Oklahoma, Colorado, Utah, and Oregon. Because his father was a sharecropper, they moved on a yearly basis and Archie never attended the same school more than one year until he arrived in High School. Having been mostly in one-room, country schoolhouses, the High School was almost like a foreign country to him. He dropped out as soon as his age allowed him to join the Navy where he served his three-year enlistment, plus one more for President Truman because the Korean War was raging and all enlistments were extended for a year. He was an Amphibious Landing Craft Coxswain and was involved in every amphibious operation in the Korean War, attached as "Ship's Company," aboard the USS Cavalier APA-37. Archie has been writing poetry most of his life. He used to write poems then throw them away because poetry did not fit his daily life. He has two published books on poetry: *Sartor's Poetry* (36 poems); and *The Collection* (525 pages). His poetry is always written in rhyme and meter. He is presently writing a Crime Fiction novel with the sub-plot in Mystery. His poem *Farmer* is dedicated to his father, Archie Lee Hoagland, born in 1880, who lived 92 years.

Carol Hogan has been writing poetry since her teens, but says she wasn't brave enough to read her poetry out loud till she reached her 50's. With that she will laugh and then proceed to read poetry that reaches into our hearts and finds those spaces left untouched and often unknown. Carol was raised on the beaches of Southern California and traveled from coast to coast until she settled in the Valley of the Sun, Phoenix, Arizona. She laughs as she cries, she roars her protests to life's indignities and brings with her a taste of what she calls, "California Hippydom". Of course this is followed with her own laughter. Carol has been a very active member of the Arizona State Poetry Society for many years. She has two self-published chapbooks of poems and has traveled to many states to read her work. Additionally, she is active in promoting and supporting new poets and those who are coming to read poetry for the first time. It is her hope that writers will step forward and bring to the stage more of their own human experience. To make this happen, Carol has hosted several open readings in the Phoenix area, one of the "Poetry in the Park – Encanto Series" ran for seventeen years (Carol's tenure was just 8 years). Carol is currently the Chair of the ASPS 2012 Fall Poetry Contest which is held in conjunction with the ASPS Fall Conference held in November.

Jim Hogan runs The Hogan School of Real Estate in Tucson. He has performed songs at many events in and around Tucson. His two CD's are "Home in Arizona" and "When I Pick up my Guitar". His poems are on these CD's. I received my Broker's license through his school.

Richard Humphries has had a TV special made about his experiences along the border with Mexico. He was interviewed by Bill O'Reilly on Fox News. My wife and I had supper with his family and saw the 30 foot tower he built to protect his family. He has written hundreds of letters to Arizona Senators and Congressmen about the plight of ranchers along the border.

Kari Infantino graduated from Gannon University with a Bachelor's in Speech and Drama and received a Master's degree at ASU. She has been a high school English teacher for 23 years at Carl Hayden High School in Phoenix, AZ. She leads the Poetry Slam there and takes part in the Poetry Central in her district every year. She is writing an adolescent novel and has written many poems and short stories. She lives in Ahwatukee. Her daughter works as the art Administrator for Tempe.

Lisamarie Jelderks was born January 30, 1969 in Portland, Oregon. She moved to Tucson in 2006 with her daughter, Annabelle, to be near her parents, Vern and Kitty Jelderks, of Marana, Arizona. She graduated from Portland State University with a Bachelor of Arts in English and Minor in Art History in 1992. She is currently employed with Bank of the West in Tucson as a Financial Service Officer and won Bank of the West's Circle of Excellence Award in 2011. She has been an active contributor to *Pinal County Lifestyles Magazine* in Casa Grande since 2010. Her novel *The Willamette Saloon Haunting: A Tuesday Brousseau Paranormal Mystery* will be released in May 2012, which is the first of a series with Imago Press.

Earl Jenson has lived in SaddleBrooke for 10 years following his retirement from the Federal Government. He has played in bands and has appeared solo as a singer-songwriter years ago, but now is a "non-performing" amateur songwriter, mainly entering lyric and song competitions or writing for local artists. Sometimes a lyric will grow into a complete song, but sometimes the "heart" of a lyric becomes a poem – he never knows which. Perhaps that makes him a lyricist-poet, or a poet-lyricist – he never knows which.

Leila Joiner publishes books through her company, Imago Press. Several of the poets in this book have used her company to publish for them.

William Killian: *All the Faces I Have Been, From the Balcony*, are two of his recent books. Both were published by Imago Press. William LaMar Killian, SR.

is an actor, poet, minister, and marriage and family therapist who loves the game of basketball. He is a member of 3 actor unions; SAG/AFTRA/AEA. He founded the ethics program at Tucson Medical Center, The Tucson Chaplains Association, and the La Casita Counseling Center at St. Phillips in the Hills Episcopal Church, Tucson, AZ.

Ann Kuperberg's *Purple Passion* was published in *African Violet Magazine*, and *Dear Wizard* was published in *Yellow Bricks and Ruby Slippers*. She was Teacher of the Year in Comstock, Michigan Public Schools. She has over 500 items published, some in *Desert Leaf* and other publications. She writes a monthly cat article for *SaddleBag Notes*.

Maggie Lawrence was born in Missouri 86 years ago. She has been writing most of the time since. After college, she went to Chicago where she met and married Bob. After several moves and four children, they found Tucson and knew this was where they belonged. For a short time, Bob established the Ugly Mug Pottery downtown and Maggie went to Library school at UA. After Bob died in 2005, her consolation is in writing poems and reading.

M.C. Little has been a resident of Arizona since 1986. She is currently employed at the VA hospital in Phoenix and has worked for the VA for over 19 years. She has participated in a few poetry workshops in Phoenix and was a business education instructor for about 10 years. She wrote the poem *Friends* after viewing television coverage of 9/11 in 2001.

Annie Maud volunteers for Golden Goose, a community thrift store. She actively participates in the SaddleBrooke-Also-Rans, is a member of the P.E.O Sisterhood, is on the Governing Board of the Vestry of her church, is a member of the SaddleBrooke Nature Club, was a former English teacher, and serves on the SaddleBrooke Architecture Landscape Committee.

Melanie McCuin graduated from Arizona State University with a BA in History in 2005. She has been published in *The Blue Guitar*, *The Salt River Review*, and *The Gila River Review*. She has placed in several local writing competitions for both poetry and fiction, including the Maricopa Community Colleges District Creative Writing Competition and the Mesa Community College Creative Writing Competition. She lives in Tempe, AZ, where she teaches Creative Writing at a local charter high school. She is the co-founder of *The Kitchenette Writer's Collective*.

Kaitlin Meadows describes herself as an artist, rebel, and an archaeologist who offers an oasis of creative play and art making at her studio Kaitlin's Creative Cottage in Tucson. She is V.P. of the Tucson Kitchen Musicians. She has been included in the anthology of *Our Spirit, Our Reality*.

Warren Miller submitted a *Arizony's Probation* written by deceased poet

Charles Badger Clark in 1910.

Debby Mitchell is a poet/writer, teacher, and desert interpreter. She was nominated for the Pushcart Prize in Poetry in 2002. She teaches university writing and ethnobotany courses. She is a desert photographer and focuses on cactus flowers that bloom. Debby continues to write about the relationships of life and nature.

Bertha E. Monroe published the book *Come to the Light*. It contains 130 poems.

Sheila Murphy: B.A. degree (magna cum laude, music/English) from Nazareth College, Kalamazoo, Michigan, Ph.D. (Education Administration and Supervision, Emphasizing Community Education, Charles Stewart Mott Fellow) from Arizona State University.

Burgess Needle's works have appeared in *Under the Radar* (UK), *Decanto* (UK), and many others. He taught English for two years in the Peace Corps. He was a school librarian for thirty years. Dominuendo Press published *Every Crow in the Blue Sky*.

Regina Lynn Nelms was born during a rare snowstorm in Tucson, AZ. She is an award winning writer and multi-media artist. As a Creative Arts Practitioner she has exhibited, lectured, and facilitated workshops on the value of the arts in wellness and healing for numerous hospitals and clinics. She is a reader for the blind and a docent at the Scottsdale Museum of Contemporary Art.

Shawnte Orion's poetry has appeared in *Georgetown Review, Juked, New York Quarterly, Sakura Review*, and other publications. He hosts popular monthly readings and is often invited as a featured reader at bookstores, bars, colleges, hair salons, museums, and laundromats.

Amy Ouzoonian is a poet, dancer, performance artist and yogi. She is co-founder of RareAzona Designs with Reuben Brock.

Bonita Papenfuss Since retiring and moving from Minnesota to Green Valley, AZ seven years ago, Bonnie is attempting to fulfill a promise made to herself to devote more time to her passion of poetry. She has a love of words and especially enjoys writing about both the perils of growing older and the beauty of the Sonoran Desert she now calls home.

Holly Parsons is the author of *Soul of a Woman A Poetic Journey in Love and Life*. This collection, 112 poems, addresses a broad range of social and justice issues from a woman's POV. She's a member of the AZ State Poetry Society and the Poetry Society of America. Poetry has taken her to Dublin, Ireland, throughout AZ and Southern CA. She is also published on several non-profit websites and magazines.

Agnes Paulsen has been writing songs with her original poems for many years, and three of them are published in a songbook for children and youth titled *May this Light Shine*. She has also self-published two songbooks. About five years ago, she met weekly with three other women who produced poems to share with each other. Having been born in Australia of Danish parents, she immigrated with them at the age of two and became a citizen of the U.S. when she was 21 years of age. Now she has lived in Tucson since 1973 and appreciates the culture so prevalent in this state.

Lyle Paulsen, for many years, met with a group of poets on Monday evenings where they critiqued each other's poems. His daughter, Ann Kozachik, published a book of his poetry in the year 2000. Lyle passed on in 2004. He told his wife, Agnes, that he wanted to be remembered as a poet.

Marge Pellegrino is an award winning author and teaching artist. Her essays, articles, and poetry have been published in regional and national publications. All her children's books are available in Korean, and her early chapter book, *Too Nice*, is also published in Polish. *Journey of Dreams* won the Judy Goddard Award for young adult literature, and is honored on nine lists including *Smithsonian Notable Books*, *Southwest Books of the Year* (2009) and *Award Commended List* (2010).

James Robert Platt has served as president of the East Valley Poets and as a board member of the Arizona State Poetry Society.

Hazel Bailey Ray, a South Carolina native, has been writing poems for over a decade, several of which have been published. She is also the author of *Stories As Medicine*, a book in which she gives her own archetypal interpretation of well-known fairytales and shares how they have played out in her life. She does workshops based on fairytales and in February 2012 did a workshop on *The Frog Prince* for the State Assembly of Church Women United along with her colleague, professional storyteller Sylvia McConico. Ms. Ray plans to publish her poems in book form at a future date.

Jennifer Reich PhD, RN, is a recent doctoral graduate of the University of Arizona College of Nursing. Jen is a nurse, poet, and storyteller. Her research explores the role of story in health promotion and healing.

Maria Rodriquez-Pope was born in San Miguel de Tucuman, Argentina. She now lives in Phoenix, AZ. She is a poet, visual artist, and writes poems in both Spanish and English. She was kind enough to translate *One God, One World, One People* into Spanish.

Larry E. Sarkis published two books on real estate formulas and has published three books in a series of five: *Our Town, the Mystery Series, The Streets of Our Town*, and *More Streets of Our Town* (available online). He has taught real estate classes across the USA. His Cowboy Auctions at National Marketing Sessions are great. Real estate exchangers know his name.

Barbara Scheidel has been involved with editing and writing since 1963. She and her husband, Roy, live in the Sahuarita area and look forward to having more time to pursue their leisure-time pursuits.

P.J. Scheidel credits Steve Miller with the title to his poem *The Man in the Door*.

Marilou Schunter is a guest poet from Culpepper, VA. She is a member of Elizabeth Doyle Solomon's Barboursville Reading Group. I attended one of their sessions and thought this poem *Mascara* was delightful. What a fun write!

Helen Spencer Schlie Born in Deford, Michigan 88 years ago, she started school the year after Lindberg flew the Atlantic, 1928. Graduated from Oxford High School (can honestly claim 4 years at Oxford). Drove Army Trucks in WW2. Owned and operated a bakery during the Rationing Years of the 40's. Did advertising and displays for JC PenneyCo, and acted as his hostess many times. (interesting stories).Opened the Mesa Temple View Bookstore in 1965 to 1990. Opened a Rare and Out of Print Bookstore at the same location in 2010 on my 87th Birthday. My husband, Walter, was a WW1 Veteran. So I am one of the few WW1 Widows in the wor;ld. One Daughter, Alnita Lester, who is a Great Grandmother, which makes me a Great Great. Have a volume of published poetry *And So It Begins* with several more volumes in the making.

Elizabeth Doyle Solomon, another guest poet, wrote *The Steering Wheel Poems*. She has written over 100,000 poems. She leads a **poetry Critique Group** for the Blue Ridge Chapter of the Virginia Writer's Club. She helped my mother get hearing aids and wrote a poem about it when the Lions Club in Tucson, AZ sent mother a set of hearing aids and my mother could hear again. They both cried. Elizabeth penned *New Ears for Virginia*.

Elaine Stamm is a member of the SaddleBrooke Writer's Club.

Mary Kay Stein was the editor for three years of *SaddleBag Notes*. She is a biomedical writer and editor, and professional photographer in Tucson. She is President of MD Communications, a medical writing, editing, and consulting company, and Desert Light Photography, a portrait and events photography company. She is the Managing *Editor of Eating Disorders Review*.

Jim Tayburn grew up on a dairy farm in central New York State and went to college in Buffalo, NY. He worked for Occidental Petroleum Corporation in sales and marketing for 37 years. Writing poetry has always been a hobby and poems are usually written for some special occasion or for some issue of the times. He has always been able to write, and, since retiring in 2005, he has been able to spend more time doing something he really enjoys.

Fred Taylor wrote *Unpredictable Outcomes* and *Ask No Questions* by Pennywse Press. If you served in Vietnam, *Unpredictable Outcomes* is a must read. Fred was a contributing writer in *Five Poets Write about Aging, Illness, and Mortality*. He is also an artist.

Bob Temple was raised at Hayden, Colorado, on a Hereford ranch. He went to Colorado State University to earn a BS and Masters in Animal Breeding. After serving in the Army, he received his PhD in Animal Genetics from Iowa State University in 1959. He taught Animal Breeding at Louisiana State and the University of Tennessee. In 1966 he took a position with the Food and Agricultural Organization in Rome, Italy. He and his family have lived in Italy, Mexico, and Ethiopia for 14 years. Their son, Greg, has lived in Prescott since 1984. Bob and Jeanenne moved to Prescott in January, 2010. He is a member of the Arizona Cowboy Poets Gathering and a life time member of Lions Club. His hobbies are writing cowboy poetry and wood turning.

Jody J. Thompson has lived in Los Angeles, Seattle, San Francisco, various parts of Ohio, and has traveled to England and Ireland. She has been published in the award winning literary magazine *SandScript* and was the recipient of the 2011 Martindale Library Award. Ms. Thompson is the publicist and contributing editor for Cairn Press.

Marsha Ward is an award-winning poet, writer, and editor whose published work includes three novels and over 900 articles, essays, columns, poems, and short stories. Her poem *My Mother's Bureau Drawer* won First Prize in three poetry contests, including the 2003 Alice Abel Literature Competition sponsored by American Mothers, Inc. Marsha also is a workshop presenter and writing teacher. Her newest novel, *Spinster's Folly*, is expected to be published in 2012.

Hawkeye Watkins grew up in Alaska. He attributes his independent spirit and self-reliance to this (and blames his Aries/Horse astrological chart – ha ha). When he was 17 he spent a year hitch-hiking across the US, living out of his backpack, going where his thumb took him that morning. He spent 10 years in the Alaska National Guard (Airborne Infantry – Recon; Medical Specialist; and Journalist). He spent 10 years in the IT field, working at places such as Microsoft, Compaq, Compuware, and CompuCom, as a Network Engineer, Technical Writer, and/or Project Coordinator. He spent 10 years as a Massage Therapist and Chi-kung (Qigong) instructor. Somewhere along the way he bought a 5 acre lot of trees, built a 6,000 sq. ft. home on it and sold it (just to see what it was like), published a fantasy genre book called *Gilbred Guteater* (for the fun of it), earned a BS in Business Management, and maybe a few other things. He finds his wanderlust has landed him in Tucson for the time being, studying internal kung-fu and psychic healing. His tale is not yet told.

Stuart Watkins collected all the poems going into this book. Stuart is a member of the Arizona State Poetry Society, Virginia State Poetry Society, The Society of Southwestern Authors, SaddleBrooke Writer's Club, and has attended several poetry club meetings in the Phoenix area. He has written poems, fiction, magazine articles and several collections of poetry since high school and has published in several national publications. He loves poetry.

mikel weisser (sic) has had such a weird, wild array of experiences that he must be a poet. He is a teacher from So-Hi, AZ. He encourages his students to write. What could be better?

Carol Christy White has been writing poetry since she first put pencil to paper, almost! Her poetry was first published in *Pegasus Junior* (the Kentucky Poetry Society's student anthology) and has been published in *Sandcutters* (Arizona State Poetry Society's quarterly journal), *Laughing Dog*, *Erete's Bloom*, *The Moon*, and other journals throughout the US. She has read her poetry in a number of venues in Arizona, Kentucky, Tennessee, Oregon, and Scotland. Christy has been active promoting poets and their poetry for a number of years. She was on the board of the Tucson Poetry Festival for five years and is currently serving as president of the Arizona State Poetry Society. She has published several chapbooks, the last published was *Proof* in 2011.

Jacequeline Williams published *Illusions of Farewell* in *ASPS Sandcutttters*, Quarterly, 2010. She published *My fingertips Braille You to Me* in The AZ State Poetry Society Annual Contest, 2010. She published *White Wings Crease the Sky* in *ASPS Sandcutters*, Quarterly, 2008.

David Willing is a transplant from Florida. He has resided in Arizona for four and a half years with his dog and cat. He attended Florida State University three years, then graduated from Southern Oregon University. He is a corporate trainer, has worked in the field of Child Welfare for nearly 20 years, but has worked as a cook, construction worker, waiter, bartender, trash collector, cabinet maker, and a host of other assorted jobs. He is an avid mountain trail runner, sculpts in wood and stone, enjoys jazz, blues, and rock-n-roll. He views many of his writings as emotional snapshots of a fleeting moment in time.

David and Judy Wood reside in Mesa, AZ, and have been married for 38 years. Both are artists, musicians, and poets. *Lazy Lizard* is their first collaboration in poetry. Judy has published one chapbook and is preparing to publish an autobiographical book of poetry. David's poems were recently featured in prints and t-shirts created by their first collaboration (a son), Chris Wood. Their other son, Jeremy Wood, is a full time musician. David and Judy wish to thank their family for bringing so much joy to their lives.

C.J. Wright is a member of the SaddleBrooke Writer's Club, an ordained minister and an international speaker. She published a book *Cameos for the Journey*. She has lived in Oregon, Washington, D.C., California, Hawaii, Missouri and Washington State.

Luis Albert Yucupicio is 18 years old, Native American, and enrolled with the Pascua Yaqui Tribe of Tucson, Arizona. He is currently a student at Pima Community College in pursuit of a Master's Degree in Social Work with a Minor in Writing. His plan is to assist other children and teens as they cope with life-threatening illness, as I have and continue to. He is currently going on 2 years and 8 months cancer free, having had a long fight with brain cancer four times since the age of 10. He was diagnosed in 2003 and relapsed in 2007, 2008, and 2009. He has had five brain surgeries and, due to these surgeries, no longer has the use of his right arm and some of his right leg. His love of writing is what has gotten him through some really rough times. He loves to write fiction and enjoys writing poetry. Writing helps him escape to a different place and time, a better place, a better time.

What a great combination of student poets, first time writers, and outstanding poets who are known throughout Arizona; some are known worldwide. I thank you all for joining me in this tribute to the 100th year of Arizona's Statehood. I tried to select a wide variety of poems and creative writing and to accept poets from all across Arizona. The title of the book is not quite accurate. There are more than 100 poets and more than 100 poems, but it reads and sounds a lot better than 112 poets and 153 poems (or whatever the total ends up being).

I want to pay tribute to Arizona State Senator Al Melvin from District 26. He has been most helpful in the attempt to establish the position of Arizona State Poet Laureate for the first time. Arizona is currently one of eight states without this position being filled.

This book has been put together with the editing and computer skills of Hawkeye Watkins, my son. He has published a book, *Gilbred Guteater*, created an instructional DVD for professional Massage Therapists, is a Technical Editor in the IT industry, and has edited several books, manuals, and websites for others. I thank him for his selfless assistance, without which the simple reality is that this book would probably not have come to be.

My idea for Arizona: 100 Years, 100 Poems, 100 Poets came as a result of my efforts to have the Governor, or the members of our Senate and House cause the position of Arizona State Poet Laureate to become a reality. Perhaps this will happen.

Again, I thank all who contributed their poems, those who prodded other poets to send in their writes, and to the outstanding poets who let me use some of their poems in this book. One of you is likely to be selected as the First Arizona State Poet Laureate.

Sincerely,

Stuart Watkins

Two Birds in Cages

Two birds in cages,
side by side.
Their songs reach each other,
but their wings may never touch.
Two birds in cages,
side by side,
each with songs to sing.
With open doors, they fly free.

Made in the USA
Charleston, SC
17 May 2012